The Cure for
Corporate Stupidity

Larry J. Bloom

D1564878

The Cure for Corporate Stupidity

Avoid the Mind-Bugs™ that Cause Smart People to Make Bad Decisions

Larry J. Bloom

Xmente
Atlanta
2012

Published in the United States by
Xmente
Suite 364D
227 Sandy Springs Place
Atlanta, GA 30328
www.xmente.com

Cover and interior design by Höhne-Werner Design, Maine, USA
www.heyneon.com

Paperback ISBN: 978–1–936678–00–6
ePub ISBN: 978–1–936678–01–3
Kindle/mobi ISBN: 978–1–936678–02–0
ePDF ISBN: 978–1–936678–03–7

LCCN: 2011939239

Publisher's Cataloging-in-Publication
(Provided by Quality Books, Inc.)

   Bloom, Larry J.
      The cure for corporate stupidity : avoid the
   mind-bugs that cause smart people to make bad decisions
   / Larry J. Bloom. -- 1st ed.
      p. cm.
      Includes bibliographical references and index.
      LCCN 2011939239
      ISBN-13: 978-1-936678-00-6
      ISBN-10: 1-936678-00-4

      1. Success in business. 2. Decision making.
   3. Corporations--Decision making.   I. Title.

   HF5386.B56 2011   650.1
                         QBI11-600191

Printed in the United States

9 8 7 6 5 4 3 2 1

Dedicated to my father, Aaron Bloom,

the quintessential advocate of Excellent Judgment.

EJ all the way!

Contents

Summary: If You Only Read One Chapter, This is It 9
Using the Book 13
    0:   Corporations and Mind-Bugs. 15
Section 1:   Understanding Mind-Bugs 25
    1:   Bugs in Our Thinking 27
    2:   How We Take Action: The Process 33
    3:   No Help from Our Brain: Brain Signals 43
    4:   The Four Mind Functions. 49
    5:   The Two Ways 55
    6:   Taking Command 59
    7:   What to Remember - Section 1 65
Section 2:   Identifying Mind-Bugs. 67
    8:   Meet the Mind-Bugs 69
    9:   Mind-Bug Reference Guide 73
    10:   The Sufficiency Dimension Mind-Bugs 79
    11:   The Accuracy Dimension Mind-Bugs 83
    12:   The Beliefs Dimension Mind-Bugs. 87
    13:   The Social Dimension Mind-Bugs 91
    14:   What to Remember - Section 2 95
Section 3:   Avoiding Mind-Bugs. 97
    15:   Defining the Problem 99
    16:   The Solution—A Path to Better Decisions 107
    17:   Step 1: Improving My Own Thinking 113
    18:   From Step 1 to Step 2: The Two Questions about the Two Ways . . 119
    19:   Step 2: Improving Interaction in Groups. 129
    20:   Step 2 Continued: The Two Ways of Interacting with Others. . . . 135
    21:   Step 3: Improving Learning and Feedback 139
    22:   Step 4: Decisions, The 30 Second Scan 145
    23:   Step 4 Continued: The Mind-Bug Debugging Process 147
    24:   Step 5: Correction 153
    25:   Step 6: Using the Path to Better Decisions 157
    26:   What Prevents the First Step? 161
    27:   The Age of Quality Thinking 163
Endnotes 169
Acknowledgements and Gratitude 177
Section 4:   Appendices 181
    A: The Steps, Tools, and Practices 183
    B: How the Book Wrote Itself 195
    C: The Research —Mind-Bugs Fundamental Themes 197
    D: References. 217
Index. 231

If You Only Read One Chapter, This is It

What were they thinking when they made that decision?

— *Anonymous Employee*

The book is written for everyone who wants to improve their decisions, help achieve better company results, decrease risk, improve teamwork, grow their careers, reduce stress, and do more with less. It is about:

1. …how leaders, managers, and employees may unknowingly make bad decisions and destroy value along the way.
2. …why many are simply unaware of the flaws plaguing some of their decisions and resist any thought that they are wrong—until it is too late.
3. …a simple, straightforward, low cost, easy-to-implement way to understand, identify, and avoid many flawed decisions.

The insights and solutions were developed based on my 30+ years of experience as a top executive of a market-leading growth company and five years of researching the work of hundreds of experts in their fields. Accordingly, I bring the unique perspective of an insider who knows that problems in corporations rarely stem from a shortfall in technical or professional expertise, but rather from a shortcoming in the "soft" skills of social interaction, communication, and self-management.

The Problem

As humans, we are hard-wired for survival. As a result, our thoughts are often out of place in the very different kinds of "survival" situations we encounter in business, as well as in modern life. But most of us are not conscious of these mismatches and the internal processes that occur in the 5-inch space between our ears. Consequently, our decisions are often not as rational as we believe, or are based on a non-conscious defective analysis of our options. The result is that our judgments and decisions often suffer in ways that could have been avoided.

Concept

Just like bugs can inhabit our computer operating systems and software applications, they can exist in human beings as well. I call these mind-bugs™. I use the term mind-bugs as a metaphor for the problems all humans experience with thinking, as a result in part of being hard-wired for survival. While my work is supported by considerable science, (See Appendix C) the technical language is not practical for most applications in business. So through the use of fresh, simple-to-grasp terms like mind-bugs, and equally straightforward practices, this book shines a spotlight on the problem and provides business-friendly tools and solutions.

One Example – Informed Leader Fallacy Mind-Bug

Whether it is a small-project team leader well down the organization hierarchy or a "C suite" executive, we deeply want to be led by people who know what they're doing and who don't have to think about it too much. So by the time we achieve a leadership position ourselves, we are good at making others feel positive about our judgment, even if there's no strong basis. But the amount of success it takes for leaders to become overconfident isn't terribly large. Some achieve a reputation for great successes when in fact all they have done is take chances that happened to work out. The fierce personal confidence and sense of infallibility that characterizes many leaders serves as a breeding ground for this mind-bug. Most decision makers will trust their own intuitions because they think they see the situation clearly. Accordingly, it causes leaders to fall into a trap of believing they are better informed than they really are. Everything is based on the appearance of being informed, rather than actual information. How long do you think that success will last if this mind-bug bites you? This book will help you avoid this mind-bug and 19 others.

First, Do No Harm

Detecting and avoiding mind-bugs is not a new process to add to an already overburdened staff. It is a low risk, low cost, easy to implement, way to go about what we already do. This book will describe how to practice mind-bug detection as part of our daily routines. Experience shows us that executives, managers, and employees often spend far more time fixing decisions that go wrong than helping them go right in the first place. And often they are merely dealing with symptoms and not getting at the real problem. This book is about helping that change. Makes sense, doesn't it?

Thought Governance

I believe we need to expand our focus on corporate governance policies to include *thought governance policies.* Thought Governance implies that we will not take our inherently faulty thinking processes for granted. We will take command of our thinking so it is not in automated control of our decisions. Corporate missions, values, governance, and human resource processes are deficient unless they pay attention to continuous improvement in the quality of individual thinking. Directors need to step up and address this critical omission. Under good Thought Governance policies, the responsibility of leadership is to create a culture where mindfulness in decision-making can thrive, to create an organization that is in command of its thinking.

Success – Why You Should Read This Book

I believe the approach provided in this book will substantially reduce risk and improve the results of your decisions. It doesn't require significant investment, burdensome compliance measures, or disproportionate expenditures of time. It is flexible and adaptable to the way we work today.

It does require practice and commitment. While losses will still occur, they will less likely be the result of poor judgment; rather they will reflect the reality that not all investments pay off.

In the next decade and beyond, I believe the single biggest determining factor of a company's competitive success will be the ability to collectively advance its quality of thinking. Eliminating mind-bugs could be the difference between sustainable performance and failure. Give these practices a try. I sense you will be glad you did.

Using the Book

Organized for a quick payoff

I I I I I ▪ ▪ ▪ ▪ ▪ ▪ ▪ ▪ ▪ I I I I I

You may choose to read the entire book, select specific chapters, skim the chapter headlines, look only at the tools organized in the appendix, or set the book down to perhaps pick up later. Do what your spirit moves you to do. No problem; the book is designed to be useful in whatever way works best for you. The key is to take a step, any step, forward. Most people don't read business books cover to cover anyway! All chapters converge on, and add depth to, a set of fundamental themes (See Appendix C). And, I made the book as short as possible. I apologize for failing to make it even shorter.

Sections of the Book

Section 1—*Understanding Mind-bugs* focuses on learning how our internal processes of thoughts, feelings, desires, and decisions work and interact. We cannot avoid mind-bugs unless we recognize what is happening inside ourselves. With this recognition the section then addresses how to improve decisions within corporations and other organizations.

Section 2—*Identifying Mind-Bugs* teaches us to name the mind-bugs so that we learn what to look for. And, we learn to do this without becoming defensive. It provides convenient and easy-to-understand reference guides that can be used immediately without reading the entire book.

Section 3—*Avoiding Mind-bugs* teaches us to how to look for mind-bugs and provides tools and practices for avoiding them. When we do this, we grow in the way we think. And, we reduce the risk of faulty decisions

Section 4 has appendices that includes a deeper dive into the underlying research and important charts and tools from throughout the book in one section. Try browsing them; you will likely continue to have "Aha! moments".

Corporations and Mind-Bugs

Having Empathy with a Complex Situation

In February 2010, auto maker Toyota announced a recall of 400,000 of its Prius hybrid vehicles following a change in "brake feeling" caused by faulty antilock braking software. But unlike the large-scale auto recalls of years past, the root of the Prius issue wasn't a hardware problem—it was a programming problem in the smart car's embedded code. The Prius had a software bug. The same year, Toyota also conducted a safety recall to address what it termed "the risk of floor mat interference with the accelerator pedals in certain Toyota models." This time the bug was not in the computer software. It was likely in their *mental* software. I call these mind-bugs.

"We Were Not Able to Stop, Think, and Make Improvements"

Akio Toyoda, the president and CEO of Toyota, issued the following statement in regards to the recalled vehicles:[1]

"Toyota has, for the past few years, been expanding its business rapidly. Quite frankly, <u>I fear the pace at which we have grown may have been too quick</u>. I would like to point out here that Toyota's priority has traditionally been the following: First; Safety, Second; Quality, and Third; Volume. <u>These priorities became confused</u>, and <u>we were not able to stop, think, and make improvements</u> as much as we were able to before, and <u>our basic stance to listen to customers' voices to make better products has weakened somewhat. We pursued growth over the speed</u> at which we were able to develop our people and our organization, and we should sincerely be <u>mindful</u> of that. I regret that this has resulted in the safety issues described in the recalls we face today ..."

Mind-Bugs

Mr. Toyoda's comments suggest that bugs don't just inhabit our operating systems, software applications, cell phones, pacemakers, power plants, and medical equipment—they exist in human beings as well. Mind-bugs are a pervasive part of human nature; they are hard-wired in our brain and highly resistant to feedback. Many problems of corporations today are not the result of software bugs or other factors that occur outside our thinking, but rather they are "self inflicted" as a result of mind-bugs—bugs in the critical *internal* processes that occur in the five inches between our ears. For example, most agree that the mortgage crisis was triggered by excessive lending to people who simply could not afford the repayment. Temporary low rate lending programs were created to entice unqualified buyers so that lender's financial performance would prosper. How did they convince themselves and their directors this was a sound practice? Look no further than mind-bugs.

Mind-Bugs at Toyota

According to the Feb. 1, 2010 *New York Times*, Toyota's slow awakening to an accelerator problem may have contributed to a deadly crash.[2]

"... It was that tragedy that forced Toyota, which had received more than 2,000 complaints of unintended acceleration, to step up its own inquiry. Only months later did the company finally appear to come to terms with the scope of the problem—after expanding a series of recalls to cover millions of vehicles around the world, incalculable damage to its once-stellar reputation for quality, and calls for Congressional hearings. ... At almost every step that led to its current predicament, Toyota underestimated the severity of the accelerator problem affecting its most popular cars. It went from discounting early reports of problems to overconfidently announcing diagnoses and insufficient fixes...."

No Lack of Intelligence

Most of us would agree that Toyota's difficulty was not due to any lack of exceptionally bright decision makers.* I propose that the problem was not that Toyota wasn't thinking. They simply weren't considering the *quality* of their thinking. They were not thinking *about* their thoughts. Their thoughts were in command of them, rather than the other way around.

Evidence of Mind-Bugs†

It is likely that some of these mind-bugs may have been at play in the tragedy at Toyota:

- Failing to treat all data equally, regardless of financial implications.
- Seeing patterns in random data where none existed.
- Making generalizations without evidence to back them up.
- Not understanding the situation as well as they thought they did.
- Defending early positions against any questions.
- Taking assumptions for granted.

---

* I recognize that Toyota is a company that displays excellence along many fronts. But, you will soon learn that all people and companies have mind-bugs. I had a choice of many examples and Toyota just happened to be on stage as I was writing this book.

† Since we all have mind-bugs, I am aware that there may be mind-bugs in my using this Toyota example as evidence of mind-bugs. That said, Toyota president Akio Toyoda's statement to Congress "These priorities became confused, and we were not able to stop, think, and make improvements as much as we were able to before" implies flaws in thinking were present.

- Failing to encourage effective critics to challenge their thinking.
- Not understanding the magnitude of their shortcomings.
- Not spending as much energy examining their position for flaws as they did defending it.
- Trying to present the most favorable picture when it wasn't true.

Mind-Bugs are all over the place—ugly, costly mind-bugs. There's a valuable lesson for all businesspeople in what happened at Toyota and countless other industrial titans. If mind-bugs can damage the reputation of a company that was once so admired, they can harm the reputation of your company too.

Having Empathy with a Complex Situation

The corporate world is changing more rapidly with each passing day. New realities requiring continual adaptation are the norm. Corporations are driven by the need to respond to rapidly improving competition through a combination of ever-increasing productivity gains. Couple this with an urgency for creativity and innovation and today's corporation often finds it is at odds with itself. Add in the public company's paradox of managing to meet quarterly expectations, while also being on the hook for long-term growth and earnings stability. It is easy to see that the judgment, decision-making, and thinking required is complex, difficult, fast-paced, and stressful. *And yet, most corporate projections assume an ideal decision maker, one who is fully informed and completely rational.*

A Breeding Ground for Mind-Bugs

This typical corporate environment is a breeding ground for mind-bugs. If we want to be aware of one cause for the recent financial carnage, Toyota's quality problems, BP's oil well disaster, and many other organizational mistakes throughout history, we should look to mind-bugs as a common thread. People simply cannot manage complex situations successfully when mind-bugs are present.

Structure is an Invitation for Struggle

If this sounds like a painful environment, unfortunately it gets worse. You see, within all organizations there is a natural structure where the thinking of some is treated as having more authority and more superiority than that of others. Employees inherently take into consideration the position and might of people with whom they deal. So no matter how noble the goals of a corporation, there is potential for struggle beneath the surface. For survival, some employees learn to play with appearances and maintain a toolkit of deceptive tricks, many without even recognizing it. For example, they may arbitrarily align themselves with the opinions of those perceived to have more power rather than support conflicting views, even when there is evidence to the contrary. Or, they may fail to help a colleague if it gives them more power. While often referred to as office politics, these are the result of mind-bugs in action.

The Status Quo Irony

But even more complexity exists. If corporations are to grow they must have a set of fixed routines to manage quality, productivity, innovation, and growth. The unintended consequence is the potential for a norm of conduct that can become set. This is the dreaded bureaucracy which most corporations experience. When this happens, thinking that challenges the status quo can be unintentionally stifled. Suggestions that would cause the company to look bad to outsiders are challenged. And, erroneous beliefs may be reinforced by transmission inside a corporate "echo chamber."

Fighting the System in Order to Improve It

The result is one of the sad ironies of corporate life. Many innovators and change agents must *fight* the system in order to improve it. While incremental improvement is of course encouraged, most transcendent achievements first have to overcome entrenched opposition from the establishment.[3] Although we delight in the success of the "eccentrics" who contribute to the advance of corporations, it is impossible to appreciate the tragedies of those who failed, not because they were wrong, but because they could not overcome the mind-bugs built into their cultural environment and of those making decisions.

Corporations are Pre-disposed to Mind-Bugs

This inherent complexity can result in a predisposition for a corporation to serve those who operate it rather than those it was originally designed to serve. Mind-bugs challenge how employees can do their best thinking in settings that don't often reward it and may inadvertently suppress it. It is a multifaceted problem and my empathy is with the leaders, managers, supervisors, and employees that must each endure the complexity, problems, stress, anxiety, and pain that frequently exist today in the corporate environment.

Not Catching all The Mind-Bugs

Any seasoned corporate executive will of course recognize some mind-bugs and take them into account. That is what we do, for example, when we apply a discount factor to a plan in order to correct for a person's over-optimism. We do the same when we ask for a neutral third-party opinion if we suspect a recommendation may be influenced by self-interest. My experience and research suggests that these corrections are too random and inexact to be as helpful as they might be.

The problem can be typified by comments from people in various corporations who tell me they must regularly deal with some of these characteristics:

- Unreasonable expectations to do more and more with fewer and fewer resources.
- Limited or no time to think about my work, let alone get it all done in a quality fashion.
- Goals and objectives are often unclear and change frequently, causing ambiguity in my work.
- Unhealthy level of internal competition, fighting for and defending individual positions.
- Internal resistance to new ideas and thinking makes it risky to bring them up.
- Decreasing levels of trust, motivation, and fairness.
- Work becoming more exhausting and less enlivening.

Most of the people I talk with, regardless of their position, do not defend this list. Rather they tell me, "YES, that is what I am dealing with, that is what I am feeling, and that is what I am thinking—somebody finally gets it!"

Invitation to a Mind-Bug

There is no one in the world whose desires are always fulfilled. There is no one in whose life everything happens according to his or her wishes, without anything unwanted happening. From time to time we all experience agitation, irritation, and disharmony that affect our decisions. And when we suffer from these miseries, we don't keep them to ourselves; we often distribute them to others as well. So the individual reaction to corporate mind-bugs can spread like a virus to produce personal mind-bugs. Then we become unwitting accomplices in generating our own poor decisions and creating misery for ourselves and others.

Human Nature

The pervasiveness of mind-bugs in corporate decisions is because they are a product of human nature—hard-wired and highly resistant to feedback. They are a function of habitual and compulsive mental processes and our attachment to them. Here is the key condition for mind-bugs:

> **Mind-bugs can exist when our non-conscious attachment to our thoughts, feelings, desires, and decisions are stronger than our ability to let go of those attachments easily.**

When this condition occurs we are in a mode of reacting to our thoughts. Mind-bugs then can affect fact gathering, analysis, insights, judgments, and decisions—and increase risk accordingly. A decision process free of mind-bugs will ferret out poor quality analysis. The reverse is not true; superb analysis is useless if it contains mind-bugs.

Mind-Bugs and Corporate Stress

Poor decisions and a great deal of psychological stress come from the rush and hurry of a turbulent mind, which jumps recklessly to unwarranted conclusions, rushes to judgments, and often is going too fast to see events and people as they truly are. Such a mind keeps the body under continual tension. It is constantly on the move—desiring, worrying, hoping, fearing, planning, defending, rehearsing, and criticizing. It cannot stop or rest except in deep sleep, when our whole body, particularly the nervous system, heaves a sigh of relief and tries to repair the damage of the day.[4]

We are not naturally aware of the wildness or uncontrollable activities of our mind. With the practices in this book we can learn to observe the flow of sensations and the origin of our thoughts and behaviors. This is the beginning of wisdom.

Knowing Better, Choosing Worse, and Causing Harm

In today's world, suggesting that someone or some entity might be exhibiting stupidity is often taken as a serious attack to be defended against and countered. That is not my intent. When I use the term Corporate Stupidity, I am not referring to intellect but rather to decisions. Unquestionably, we have all seen exceedingly bright people make stupid decisions. Certainly, I readily admit to exhibiting my own stupidity. The problem is that humans are not naturally aware of their internal decision-making processes. As you will see, that lets mind-bugs have their influence.

Defining Corporate Stupidity

Corporate Stupidity refers to decisions that occur in a corporate environment that:

- Result in harm to one's self, to another, or to both
- Destroy value to the corporation
- Could reasonably have been avoided

This provides a straightforward definition of Corporate Stupidity. We can test any decision against three criteria. Was there a behavior? Did it cause harm? Could the result reasonably have been avoided? Said another way: A stupid decision is made by someone who could have known better, chose worse, and thus caused harm.[5] This is the kind of stupidity this book is targeting.

What about Greed and Power?

Why would anyone or any group consciously harm others or destroy value? Greed and power come to mind. But this book is not about those who knowingly destroy long-term value for their own personal gain. There is plenty written about those crooks and predators. This book is about why people—leaders, managers, and employees—non-consciously harm the company and destroy value along the way. It is about why many are simply unaware of the huge negative impact of some of their decisions and resist any thought that they are wrong—until it may be too late.

What about Governance?

Although governance reforms may help shield companies (and the economy) from the destructive impulses of some decision makers,[6] I propose that many corporate problems and meltdowns are driven by deeply embedded mind-bugs. Those will not go away by themselves, no matter how strongly companies are regulated.

To the extent we succumb to mind-bugs we will be of little value to a company who wants employees who can systematically pursue important goals, recognize and analyze significant problems, communicate essential meanings, and assess their own performance on the job.

Hopefully by now you can see that even with a book entitled *The Cure for Corporate Stupidity* I am not out to bash corporations. OK, I must admit that is tempting and it might sell books, but it does not serve my purpose. On the contrary, I have great admiration for the contribution of corporations to the world's economy and standard of living, as well as empathy for the tremendous complexity of their internal environments.

I I I I **I I ▄ ▄▄ ▄▄ ▄▄ ▄ I I** I I I

**Risk is not something that corporations avoid;
it is something they manage.
Mind-bugs increase risk. Avoiding mind-bugs reduces risk.**

Section 1: Understanding Mind-Bugs

We cannot avoid mind-bugs unless we recognize what is happening inside ourselves.

I I I I I ▪ ▪ ▪ ▪ ▪ ▪ ▪ ▪ ▪ I I I I I

Section Contents by Chapter:

1. Bugs in Our Thinking
2. How We Take Action: Our Internal Processes
3. No Help from Our Brain: How We are Wired for Survival
4. Four Mind Functions: Four Things Our Mind Communicates
5. The Two Ways: Reacting or Reflecting
6. Taking Command of Our Thinking
7. What to Remember

Note to Scientists, Physicians, and other Professionals

I highly respect your efforts in the different disciplines of biology, physics, chemistry, neuroscience, critical thinking, psychology, psychiatry, philosophy, spirituality, and more. I respectfully ask for your indulgence with this model and its liberties with very deep, technical, and personal subjects. It was by way of discovering my own faulty thinking that I decided to attempt the challenge of simplification for business purposes. That said, I welcome and encourage challenge to these ideas and approaches as part of continuous improvement and personal growth.

Chapter 1: Bugs in Our Thinking

*The first step is an intuition, and it comes with a burst;
then difficulties arise. It is then that 'Bugs'—as such little
faults and difficulties are called—show themselves.*

— Thomas Edison 1878

The invention of the term "bug" is often erroneously attributed to Grace Hopper, a computer scientist and United States Navy Rear Admiral. As a pioneer in the field of computer programming, her work led to the development of one of the first modern programming languages. Hopper publicized the cause of a malfunction in an early electromechanical computer. A typical version of the story goes like this:

> In 1945, when Hopper was released from active duty, she joined the Harvard Faculty at the Computation Laboratory where she continued her work on the Mark II and Mark III computers. Operators traced an error in the Mark II to a moth trapped in a relay, coining the term *bug*. This bug was carefully removed and taped to the log book September 9th, 1945 (see picture).

The entry reads: "First actual case of bug being found." The word went out that they had "debugged" the machine and the term "debugging a computer program" was born.

Photo of what is possibly the first real bug found in a computer
Courtesy of the Naval Surface Warfare Center, Dahlgren, VA, 1988.

Software Bugs

A software bug is the common term used to describe a fault in a computer system that produces an incorrect or unexpected result. But per the quote from Thomas Edison, the use of the term "bug" to describe inexplicable defects has been a part of engineering jargon for many decades. It predates computers and computer software. Most bugs arise from mistakes and errors made by people—human beings who are making decisions. And sixty-plus years after Grace Hopper's discovery, bugs are still with us, showing no sign of going extinct.

Mind-Bugs

Bugs don't just inhabit our computers and software—they exist in human beings as well.

Mind-bugs are a pervasive part of human nature. They are hard-wired in our brain and highly resistant to feedback. Many problems of corporations today are not the result of factors that occur outside our thinking, but rather they are "self inflicted" as a result of mind-bugs—bugs in the critical *internal* processes that occur in the five inches between our ears.

The Paradox

Today's business environment is conducive to mind-bugs. Think about it. In most organizations, demand on employees exceeds capacity. People are busier today than they have ever been. And technology has created an environment where multi-tasking is the norm both at home and at work. Companies are investing to improve individual productivity, to accomplish more with fewer people.

The paradox is that the success of any organization is a function of the quality of the thinking done within it. Employees are being paid specifically for their thinking, and yet corporations are doing little to improve the *quality* of their thinking. While many companies invest in training, it is my observation and experience that far too little (if any) goes to improving thinking processes.

How Mind-Bugs Create Problems

We all have thoughts. But few of us think *about* our thoughts. Mind-bugs can emerge when we don't take time to assess our thoughts. It's that simple. Only when we become aware of the impact of our thoughts, feelings, desires, and influences can we make impartial decisions. Otherwise, we may get lucky but we will be unaware of true cause and effect. If we don't practice mind-bug detection, the mind-bug thought patterns may sneak up and bite us. Then we will make decisions that cause harm to ourselves and others or destroy value in our company and never even know why.

How We Behave at Work When Mind-Bugs are Lurking

The behaviors listed below are evidence of buggy thinking that leads to corporate stupidity. These are pervasive thoughts and behaviors that can be found in nearly every corporate decline and failure. Perhaps you have noticed them at work in your own company.

- We believe we have figured out the way things are—regardless of evidence to the contrary—and don't grasp the contradictions between our view and reality.
- We justify conclusions that serve our interests and develop skills of selective evidence-finding and debate.
- We do not see the limitations in our point of view and want to win arguments without examining whether there are problems with our own thoughts.
- We place blame anywhere but with our own thinking and look back after the fact and defend our decisions with platitudes like: "I wish I knew then what I know now," or "It seemed like a good idea at the time."
- We develop complex, defensive, and inflexible habits which are not discussable. Worse, to consider discussing them is not discussable.
- We are blind to our own limitations and blind to the fact that we are blind.

Why Haven't Mind-Bugs Already Been Eradicated?

You would think that after many decades and volumes upon volumes of writing about business, managers and executives would avoid the costly errors that can sink a company. But that's not how it works.

First of all, change is hard; it is easier said than done. That's because the very mind-bugs that are the problem cause us to resist change. Change the way we think? Our mind-bugs tell us there is absolutely nothing wrong with the way we think.

Secondly, we need a fresh approach to minimize the impact of mind-bugs. And, the truth is, everyone is stretched so thin with the requirements of their job (or frequently, more than one) that they are often not open to learning a new way of thinking about business. They simply don't have the time, energy, or motivation.

Third, this new way might be considered warm and fuzzy. No one in the corporate world seems to have time for warm and fuzzy. This is because companies like the hard stuff and have a built-in bias against the soft stuff. In my experience, problems in corporations rarely stem from a shortfall in technical or professional expertise, but rather from a shortcoming in the "soft" skills of social interaction, communication, and self-management behaviors. To solve the problem of poor decision making, mind-bugs must be addressed. That's an internal fix. Many will consider it soft.

And, one more constraint: All change comes ultimately from the human brain. Understanding the brain and mind spans the very different disciplines of biology, physics, chemistry, neuroscience, critical thinking, psychology, psychiatry, philosophy, and spirituality. The complexity of connecting these worlds with a common language suitable for business use is vexing. That is the challenge I am undertaking.

The Solution: Take Command of Our Thinking

The solution to preventing mind-bugs sounds simple. It's all about learning to take command of our thinking. The problem is that our thoughts get in the way. You will soon find out that *we take command of our thinking in the mental space between stimulus and response.*

Mental Breakpoint and Debugging

In the technology world, software programmers insert a breakpoint[7] to suspend execution of a program at certain points in order to look for bugs in the oftentimes millions of lines of code. To take command of our thinking, we need to do the same by inserting a mental breakpoint to debug our thoughts. It requires developing a personal awareness of problems in our thinking. If we don't make a mindful assessment of our thinking quality, any response may be plagued with mind-bugs. With a mental breakpoint we become aware of problems in two areas:

- Flaws in what input we use to make decisions.
- Flaws in how we make decisions.

These errors are caused by the unknown presence of mind-bugs which are defined in a simple manner and organized in later chapters. Learning about these will lead to detection and avoidance.

The Process

Detecting and avoiding mind-bugs is not a new process to add to an already overburdened staff. It is a low risk, low cost way to go about what we already do. This book will describe how to use this knowledge to practice mind-bug detection as part of our daily routines.

Somehow in today's world we have acquired the idea that the mind works best when it runs at top speed.[8] Yet, operating all-out at maximum speed is not healthy, nor is it conducive to making the highest quality decisions. A mind that is always racing lacks time even to complete a thought, let alone to check on the quality of its own thinking. It just coughs up whatever thoughts it can; the more the better. And the faster it cranks, the more likely it is to overheat, misfire, jam, and even shut down. This provides a fertile environment for the growth of mind-bugs.

Taking the Path Requires Courage

It takes courage to challenge our own thoughts. You will soon see that it is a struggle among different parts of the brain. The real issue is that most of us do not notice our thoughts. We are out of touch with ourselves and it can be debilitating. It's like breathing carbon monoxide. You can't see it or smell it, but it can harm or kill you just the same.

Blocked by Our Own Beliefs

We all hold unrecognized beliefs that block the path to sound decisions.[‡] Once we are enthralled by our beliefs, mind-bugs cause the truth to be hard to see and hear. A misguided belief left untamed will corrupt decisions and choices.

Improve the Quality of Your Thinking

Read on to learn how to improve the quality of your thinking. I dare to suggest your world may never be the same.

---

‡ "People do not hold questionable beliefs simply because they have not been exposed to the relevant evidence. Erroneous beliefs plague both experienced professionals and less informed lay people alike." Gilovich, Thomas. *How We Know What Isn't So: the Fallibility of Human Reason in Everyday Life.* New York: Free, 1993. Print.

How We Take Action: The Process

*There always remains in any human operation,
the basic central thing which you cannot understand
—because it is you.*

— *Alan Watts*

Humans face a constant stream of decision making. But, it is even more demanding in the business world because the stream is amplified due to the increased frequency with which we meet and interact with people, plan and conduct our activities, evaluate performance, draw conclusions, or pass judgments. Business decisions also have more ambiguity due to the options and tradeoffs that usually exist. And, they are under the pressure of time constraints as well. While sound decisions are of vital importance in the business world, few are aware of the internal human processes that lead to making them. Accordingly, our internal process itself can hide error-inviting mind-bugs that affect decision quality. Understanding the process is the first step to improvement. That is the primary purpose of Section 1. This chapter introduces Figure 2-2 *The STAR Model*™, which provides a simplified view of how we take action. The acronym STAR stands for STimulus And Response (response = action).

Stimulus

Every action we take begins with some type of stimulus. That is to say, something happens either in our external or internal environment that provides information to our brain by way of our sensory system. We tend to think about our senses in terms of sight, hearing, touch, smell, and taste. But sensory receptors also can detect other stimulus such as pain, balance, temperature, motion, direction, position, time, hunger, and more. Much of the external stimuli in business are events of hearing, reading, or seeing something. Internally, the pain when those events are perceived as threats plays an important role as stimuli.

A Flood of Information

Consider that at any given moment, our five senses are taking in more than 11,000,000 pieces of information.[9] The most liberal estimate is that people can process consciously about 40 pieces of information per second. Think about it: we take in 11,000,000 pieces of information a second, but can process only 40 of them consciously.[10] What happens to the other 10,999,960? It would be terribly wasteful to design a system with such incredible sensory acuity but very little capacity to use the incoming information. Fortunately, we do make use of a great deal of this information outside of conscious awareness.

Non-Conscious Information Processing

As you read this book your senses are flooded with input. You can probably hear many sounds like the ticking of a clock, hum of the air conditioner or heater, nearby conversations, and the notice of an email or text arriving. You can see not only the words on this page, but also the page number and footnotes, your hands holding the book, the surfaces and objects beyond the book. You can feel the weight of the book and the pressure of your body against the seat of your chair. Let's not forget the aroma of coffee, the perfume of another person, and the hunger you might sense as it approaches lunch time. And all this assumes you are sitting in a quiet spot by yourself as you read.

Filtering the Information

How do we make sense of the incredible number of the competing stimuli that reach our senses? We are able to do so because we have non-conscious filters that examine the information reaching our senses that determine what to admit to consciousness.[§] The non-conscious mind is kind of like computer programs that scan the internet on their own. Then they alert us by e-mail or text message when it comes across information that is of interest to us. Part of our mind can scan what is not the focus of our attention and alert us when it determines something is important. How it determines what is important can be a problem as our non-conscious filter gathers information outside of awareness, interprets it, evaluates it, feels and selects.[11] Our internal filter programming can have bugs just like any computer program.

Automaticity

The non-conscious processes of our brain are automatic. Scientists refer to this as automaticity.[12] Automatic thoughts and behaviors are ones that occur efficiently, without the need for conscious guidance or monitoring. Most of our thoughts and behaviors tend to be automatic or have automatic components, and for good reason. These processes are fast, allowing us to do things like drive to work without having to think about how to drive and which turns to take. They are why we can think about other things as we drive. But, much of our behavior in social life is also unconsciously automatic. There is strong scientific evidence that people can respond automatically and unthinkingly in many situations; to facial expressions, body gestures, hints about a person's sex, ethnicity, or sexual orientation, information about someone's hostility or cooperativeness, and a variety of other social stimuli.[13] For example, words can automatically and non-consciously come out of our mouth before we have had a chance to think. And sometimes we later regret saying what we did. Non-conscious automatic processes are also where habits and patterns of thought reside,

---

§ Although there is some disagreement on the exact location of the filter in the attentional system, there is agreement that the filter operates largely outside of conscious awareness. Conscious control over the setting of the filter is not perfect. The desire to attend to something sometimes fails, such that our attention is drawn to precisely what we are trying to ignore. Wilson, Timothy D. *Strangers to Ourselves: Discovering the Adaptive Unconscious.* Cambridge, MA: Belknap of Harvard UP, 2002. Print.

where they form without our knowledge and conscious awareness that such processing occurs.[14]

A Blessing and a Curse

There is a bit of "good, bad, and occasionally ugly" about these processes. Certainly, there is a huge benefit in that we don't have to be aware of everything going on beneath our conscious processes. They are why we can learn to drive a car, hit a golf ball, use a computer and cell phones or play a musical instrument. But, most of us are not aware of the internal processes that occur, even when we believe we make conscious choices. You see, when we are not conscious about making decisions to take action, we are not there to know we are not there![15] And neuroscientists have determined that our non-conscious processes control over 95% of our perception and behavior with no need for conscious awareness[16]—maybe even more.

The Major Task of the Brain is Survival

The brain is a biological organ, a physical object weighing in at about three pounds. It is the gray matter inside our skull. In simplified terms, the major task of the brain is survival;¶ that is, to produce action without thinking so that our brain survives. In fact, survival is referred to as the organizing principle of the brain. All of the processes presented are connected to these very survival principles. To achieve this noble purpose the brain develops automatic non-conscious hard-wired circuits that produce a range of activities, such as executing the biological processes that keep us alive and quickly and automatically reacting to threats with the "fight or flight response",[17] the instant reaction shown in Figure 2-2. They are why we automatically duck if something is thrown at our head or may instantly back away from something perceived as dangerous or threatening.

It makes sense when we think about the evolution of humans. Our early ancestors needed above all else to instantly react in order to survive. Evolutionary-based survival programming is actually quite ingenious, helping us in a million ways every day. And, we don't even have to consciously think about it.[18] You will learn, however, that some of these non-

---

¶ "To be sure, the human brain is a bizarre device, set in place through natural selection for one main purpose – to make decisions that enhance reproductive success and survival." Gazzaniga, Michael S. Human: the Science behind What Makes Us Unique. New York: Ecco, 2008. Print.

conscious programmed patterns can actually result in errors of interpretation of what is happening right now. When that happens, mind-bugs can lead us to make faulty decisions without realizing it.

The Major Task of the Mind is Awareness

According to Merriam-Webster's dictionary, "the mind is the element or complex of elements in an individual that feels, perceives, thinks, wills, and especially reasons; the organized conscious and non-conscious adaptive mental activity of an organism." It is not a physical object or organ like the brain. In very basic terms, our mind is our personal experience of awareness.[19] Different than our brain, our mind produces thoughts, feelings, desires, and decisions as shown in Figure 2-1. These mental representations are assembled non-consciously, but the feelings they produce are accessible to the conscious mind.

Figure 2-1

The Intimate Connection of the Functions of our Mind

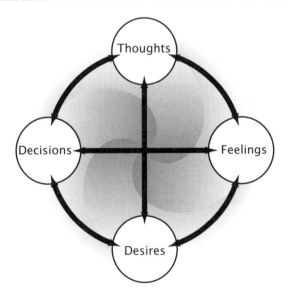

The Intimate Connection

Our thoughts are intimately connected to the feelings, desires, and decisions that occur in our mind.[20] Each of these functions continually interacts with and influences each other, based on signals from the brain. You cannot separate one from the other. Our thoughts, feelings, desires, and decisions keep rattling around in our heads with no conscious monitoring on our part. We mostly just accept them as they surface and don't question their validity. Nothing can be more important than being able to choose what we think,[21] feel, desire, and decide. The way we view our world and ourselves is wrapped up in these choices. The ancestor of every destructive action is a faulty thought, feeling, desire, or decision. Once these have been triggered, it is difficult to turn them off.

Always On

Sometimes our conscious mind may interpret that thoughts, feelings, desires, and decisions just emerge now and then. The fact is that our non-conscious mind and its processes are always on.[22] It constantly uses an internal barometer to interpret events (specific stimuli) as being important or not, good or bad, safe or dangerous, desirable or unwanted, and pleasurable or dis-pleasurable. The brain categorizes the information it receives to provide meaning and stores the mental representations it creates. For example, another person may be right in front of us but we do not just see her. We see our mental representation or idea of her. And based on that model created by our mind, we cast our judgments. It is well-documented scientifically that our mental representations are not always accurate. You might be beginning to get the picture; there are many opportunities for mind-bugs.

Consciousness

Conscious processes are where we exercise free will to direct our attention, think and reason, and make choices. Just like non-conscious processes, conscious thinking can be considered an evolutionary adaptation for survival. That's because one thing the non-conscious mind cannot do is anticipate what will happen tomorrow. Among the major functions of consciousness are the abilities to anticipate, mentally simulate, and plan.[23] An animal that has a concept of the future and past and is able to reflect on these time periods at will is in a better position to make effective plans than one that does not. That provides a tremendous survival advantage. But most of us don't appreciate that when we conjure up possible future events, our non-conscious mind has a major influence and role. Since it is programmed to look for threats based on mental representations, these threats can invade our conscious mind. How do we know which is which if we don't examine our thinking for mind-bugs? This problem likely underlies some of the most disastrous decisions in business and in mankind.

Describing Consciousness

Consider for a moment how hard it is to describe the nature of our conscious experience. It is difficult for the simple reason that we cannot observe conscious states directly in anyone but ourselves. If someone said, "Think of the ocean," you could easily do so. But you have no way of knowing if your mental image is anything like mine.

The bottom line is that scientists recognize that we know less than we think we do about our own minds, and exert less control over our own minds than we think. That suggests that hiding places for mind-bugs abound. And yet we retain some ability to influence how our minds work. That suggests we can learn to avoid them.

How We Take Action

As a result of the interaction of brain and mind *The STAR Model* in Figure 2-2 summarizes and simplifies three types of actions (responses) that we take:

- *Instant Reaction* occurs because our brain perceives a threat and triggers instant survival reactions. We fight, we flee, or we freeze, all without conscious thought. Our blood pressure automatically increases along with our heart rate as our non-conscious processes get us prepared. You will soon learn that this can be a big problem when the perceived threat is of a social and not physical nature.
- *Habitual Action* is the result of non-conscious processes that allow us to have the freedom to take action without thinking. An important part of personality is the ability to respond in quick, habitual ways to the social world. But, just as a golf swing can become ingrained with either good or bad habits, so can our ways of processing information about the physical and social world. Once bad habits of thought form they are difficult to dislodge. They continue in our non-conscious and can lead to flawed decisions and actions.

- *Initiated action* occurs when we consciously direct our attention to think, reason, and choose. But, it makes little sense to imagine what it would be like to have only a conscious mind, because consciousness itself is dependent on and constantly influenced by mental processes that occur out of view. We couldn't be conscious without a non-conscious mind. Just as what we see on the screen of a computer could not exist without a sophisticated system of hardware and software operating inside.[24] And we all know that software can have bugs.

Figure 2-2

The STAR Model™: STimulus And Response
How We Take Action

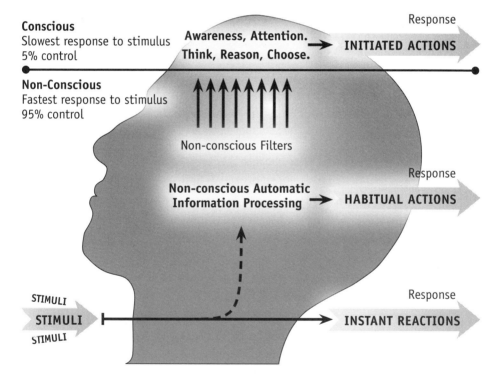

Conscious
Slowest response to stimulus
5% control

Awareness, Attention.
Think, Reason, Choose.

Response
INITIATED ACTIONS

Non-Conscious
Fastest response to stimulus
95% control

Non-conscious Filters

Non-conscious Automatic
Information Processing

Response
HABITUAL ACTIONS

STIMULI
STIMULI
STIMULI

Response
INSTANT REACTIONS

Bottom Lining Section 1

The balance of Section 1 further explains how the areas of the brain and mind interact and how problems in thinking can unknowingly occur. But the bottom line is that any event can trigger our mind and brain to react. For survival, when a threat is perceived the survival processes of our brain take priority over those of our mind, resulting in unexamined thoughts, feelings, desires, and decisions. Over time, the consequence can be an accumulation of faulty beliefs, biased judgments, and compulsive habits of thinking.

Exercise

This exercise requires only 60 seconds and demonstrates the incessant chatter that occurs in our mind and what little control we have over it. It will give you an advantage that most do not have at work when they are making decisions—a quiet space.

Find a quiet space and have a way to time one minute. Your goal is to have no thoughts of any kind enter your mind for one minute—60 brief seconds. Sounds easy, right? All you need to do is take a few deep breaths, relax, and start timing. The moment you have a thought, stop, note the elapsed time, and write down the thought. See how far you can get and what thoughts are invading your mind on their own. After all, you are just asking your mind to take a back seat for 60 seconds.

Not so easy, huh? Our mind is a thought-generating machine that just does not want to stop. It has difficulty not generating thoughts to fill a void, so we must be careful which of our thoughts we trust.

And notice, if you have the immediate thought not to do this exercise, welcome to your mind-bugs.

We are frequently in error, but rarely in doubt.

— *E. Langer, Professor of Psychology, Harvard University*

No Help from Our Brain: Brain Signals

You can check out anytime you want, but you can never leave.
— *Felder, Henley, Frey; from The Eagles' song, "Hotel California"*

I firmly believe the business world is largely filled with good people trying to make rational ethical decisions. Of course, there are the exceptions. However, the overwhelming majority of the business people I know all have good intentions. But, they inherently struggle because they are limited to using human brains—brains that are hard-wired in a way that makes it challenging to formulate wise decisions under the pressures faced at work. Furthermore, it makes it challenging to be aware of our own internal challenges!

The Human Brain is Hard-wired for Survival

The scientific study of the human brain is starting to provide underlying insights that can be applied in the real world. The simple fact is that we are living with brains that were formed thousands of years ago when daily survival was the name of the game.

Programmed to React to Perceived Threats

Our brain is a biological organ designed for survival and is programmed to react to threats.[25] For gaining an initial understanding of mind-bugs, the most relevant threat is anything that causes the brain to trigger fear, an emotional reaction which is a biochemical human response.[26] The primitive humans that had this reaction had a better chance of survival and passed on those genes to future generations up to the present.

The Fear Reaction

The fear reaction helped our distant ancestors survive dangers, for example, by freezing and not attracting a predator's attention. You may have heard of this reaction known as the fight or flight response,[27] in which the body prepares itself to either enter combat, run away, or hide. As a result of evolution, fear is a universal biological emotion generated by the human brain and experienced in a similar fashion by people across all cultures. It is an automatic response whose basis is critical to survival. It is part of us.

Fear Pathways

The fear pathways have been widely studied, initially through animals and more recently through brain-imaging studies in humans. Research strongly suggests that the amygdala is the fear center of the brain. It is part of the limbic system, a primitive part of the brain common to many animals. It has a direct pathway that leads to rapid reaction to relatively simple stimulus or input. The fear reaction unleashes a cascade of chemicals that can be measured in the skin, heart rate, blood pressure, and in the brain, engaging specific regions over others.[28] The fear reaction instantaneously gets our body ready to fight, freeze, or flee.

Fear Takes Biological Priority Over Rational Thinking

The emotion of fear travels along the brain's "highest speed connections with the greatest bandwidth" reserved for information that takes biological priority over measured thinking. This survival mechanism ensures that intense, emotionally-laden events get attended to immediately.[29] The consequence is that other regions of our brain are de-emphasized and react more slowly when a fear response is triggered, allowing reflective thinking in our mind to get emotionally hijacked by our brain. When hijacking occurs we are truly not in command of our thinking. We can only react, because to our brain, fear is far more powerful than reason. Once the fear reaction has occurred in the brain, it is difficult for the mind to turn it off. You will see that it requires some sort of intervention or interruption.

Pardon Me, My Mind Just Got Hijacked By My Brain[30]

Under emotional stimulation the brain triggers the release of chemicals such as cortisol and adrenaline that immediately change the way we think, feel, and act. If you have ever had a hard time calming down after a fear reaction, you have experienced this—and most everyone has.

Evolution's Dirty Trick

Although the fear reaction is essential to our survival, in modern humans it can also be disruptive. That's because evolution has resulted in the development of social fears. For example, if you have ever given a speech to a large crowd you likely will have experienced what many refer to as butterflies in your stomach or nervousness. This sensation is the result of the release of a flood of chemicals by a prehistoric part of the brain. You probably also noticed an increased heart rate and blood pressure as the fight or flight reaction kicked in. Since this happens automatically you may not be consciously aware of any specific fear.

You may also be compelled to deny your fear to others, as part of the fear reaction is to hide your weaknesses. Social fears in this case may include the fear of rejection, humiliation, judgment, criticism, or not being good enough.[31] If the fear is strong enough, you might flee by avoiding giving speeches in the future.

The Human Brain at Work at Work

Research strongly suggests that the reactions of the brain are profoundly shaped by social interaction. This can present enormous challenges to employees, managers, and decision makers. Although a job is often regarded as a purely economic transaction where people exchange their labor for currency, the brain experiences the workplace as a social system equated with survival.[32] For example, when people realize that they might compare unfavorably to someone else, the fear reaction is often triggered.[33]

Key Organizational Social Threats

1. Social Status[34]

We are biologically programmed to care about social status because it favors survival in our social environment.[35,36] Values have a strong impact on status. An organization that appears to place a high value on titles is ripe to stimulate fear in those that are of lesser title. That is why we can't think clearly when someone discounts our input because of being at a lesser status. Similarly, organizations that position people against one another based on the belief that it leads to better long term results reinforce the fear response. The mere phrase *can I offer you some advice* may register as *you are a problem,* and invite the fear reaction. It is like hearing threatening footsteps in a dark alley, words are lost as the logic circuits shut down to provide energy to our response to this perceived threat. This is certainly a problem if it happens in a performance review.

2. Ambiguity

When our brain perceives uncertainty or confusion it flashes an internal danger signal and the fear reaction is aroused. Even a small amount of uncertainty generates a reaction in the brain, taking attention away from the current task and forcing a fear response. It is like having your computer freeze. Until it is resolved it is difficult to focus on other things. Larger, more personal uncertainties, like not knowing if your job is secure, can be incapacitating. Uncertainty registers as something that must be corrected and triggers the fear reaction until one can feel comfortable again.[37] That is why people crave certainty by nature.

3. Control

The degree of control available to employees determines if a fear response will be triggered.[38] A perception of reduced control, for example when not being able to exercise routine decisions without perceived overinvolvement of a manager or supervisor, can easily generate fear. It is because we perceive not being in control of our own destiny. We may get defensive, attack with "social network" communication, become unmotivated or even quit. It can develop into a big organizational problem.

4. Trust[39]

Fruitful collaboration depends on healthy relationships. In the brain, each time we meet somebody new we automatically make a quick friend-or-foe distinction. We then shade our experiences with this person accordingly. When the person is perceived as different, or one who must be competed with, survival circuits may be triggered. Withholding information or backstabbing may be some of the results.

5. Fairness[40]

When events are perceived to be unfair, the survival circuits are triggered in the brain. That's because fairness matters to humans[41] and unfairness is perceived to be a threat. And once the threat response is turned on, it can be so powerful that some people are willing to fight or die for causes involving justice, fairness, equality, and the like. When people in organizations have perceptions of unfairness, the result is a lack of trust, along with a decline in motivation, cooperation, and collaboration.

Organizational Threats Lead To Mind-Bugs

Under any type of perceived threat, be it physical or social, the fear reaction may be triggered. Under this condition, the brain loses its ability to correctly interpret subtle clues from the environment, reverts to familiar behaviors, loses some of its ability to perceive relationships and patterns, and tends to overreact in a phobic way.[42] These are all mind-bugs. When they connect in ways that result in faulty decisions it is like a bug in our internal computer software—a mind-bug.

Exercise

Think of a recent time when you experienced an emotional response to a situation at work whether anger, irritation, frustration, impatience, disengagement, or the like.

Then:

1. Identify which of the five social threats apply to this situation.

2. *Recall the sensation you felt as a result of the release of chemicals by the brain.*

3. *Who else was involved and how did they act?*

4. *How did you respond?*

5. *How could you both have taken command of your thinking?*

**At work, each day is filled with moments of perceived survival.
So, much of the time,
our brains hijack our rational decision-making process.**

The Four Mind Functions

A man is but the product of his thoughts
—what he thinks, he becomes.

— *Mahatma Gandhi*

Thoughts and Thinking

Thoughts are the forms created in our mind, rather than the forms perceived through the five physical senses. They happen without our permission. For our model, thoughts result from the action of our mind to automatically create meaning of the events of our lives.[43] They are the running narrative, opining, judging, commenting in the background all day long.[44] "I like this, I don't like that, I want this or don't want that, she is so fun, he is so boring—". Thoughts continually tell us: "This is what is going on. You need to notice this and be aware of that. This is how it makes sense to interpret this situation."[45] And finally, thoughts are the constant mental noise that you experienced in the first exercise.

Then there is thinking. Thinking is an intentional mental activity that may interrupt or examine our thoughts. Or it may just remain totally under the influence of our thoughts. In common language, thinking covers numerous different psychological activities.[46] It is sometimes a synonym for "tending to believe," especially with less than complete confidence. *"I think we will meet our forecast, but I am not sure."* At other times it represents the degree of attentiveness. *"I did it without thinking."* It may refer to something outside the immediate environment. *"All this work made me think of taking a vacation; I can just see myself on the beach."* And, it is a way of reasoning or judgment. *"To my thinking, this is not a good idea."*

But, just because someone has a thought does not make it true.[47] When mind-bugs are present, thinking can become faulty. *We may not understand our thinking for what it is and more importantly, what it is not.*

Feelings and Emotions[48]

The purpose of feelings and emotions is to monitor or evaluate the meanings created by our thoughts. For our purposes, emotions are defined as brain states that generate sensations in our body.[49] Feelings are the names we give to the mental representations we assign to those body sensations as we personally interpret them. They allow neural processes to give rise to conscious content and make them meaningful.

One would not mistake seeing for hearing but the same cannot be said for thinking and feeling.

Thoughts and Feelings

Every thought has a feeling attached to it. With our feelings, we evaluate how positive and negative things are, given the meaning provided by our thinking. The feeling function continually tells us: This is how you should feel about what is happening right now. For every positive thought the mind "believes," the mind naturally tends to generate an upbeat feeling to fit it. Conversely, for every negative thought, the mind tends to generate a downbeat feeling. These become future patterns we respond to without thinking. For example, if we only expect to be attacked when presenting a budget, legitimate questions will appear to be assaults and we will have the urge to feel and react defensively.

We experience joy and frustration, happiness and anxiety, passion and indifference because we give meaning to every situation we experience and connect it to our feelings. The meaning we create may be grounded in insight or it may be a dysfunctional interpretation of reality. When feelings arise, they so quickly overtake us that we hardly notice. They happen faster than our conscious ability to think. Then, under the control of our feelings, we make decisions to take actions which may cause harm and destroy value. When mind-bugs are present, feelings can become faulty. In the moment of reacting, *we may not understand our feelings for what they are and more importantly, what they are not.*

Desires or Wants

Desire allocates energy to our decisions to take action or not. It continually tells us: "This is worth getting—go for it." Or it may say: "Not worth it, don't bother, whatever." Therefore, when we are forced to do things we do not perceive as "wantable," our desire and hence our energy and motivation are low. For example, if our desire and motivation to follow the CEO's direction for a new program is low, we will give it lip service. We might believe we are giving it support, but we only fool ourselves. Most everyone else knows we are faking it.

Desire originates in the non-conscious regions of our mind, and often we can feel it well before it emerges into consciousness. It stirs us up with all types of feelings, from vague discontent to excitement and anticipation. After gathering enough force, desire emerges into our conscious mind and then begins to demand expression in the form of decisions. Advertisers are well aware of this process—create enough desire and consumers will decide to buy their products. When mind-bugs are present, desires can be unfounded. *We may not understand our desires for what they are and, more importantly, what they are not.*

Decisions

The function of decisions is to make our mind up to do something, such as initiate a chosen action. The action may come immediately after the decision, or a while later, or it may be turned into an internal belief. For example, a CEO's desire to meet Wall Street's expectations can be so great that he forms an internal belief that questionable balance sheet maneuvers are ethical and thus fails to provide transparency.

Decisions are the result of our mind at the wheel, directing our life by way of the interaction of our thoughts, feelings, and desires. Some decisions are conscious and others are non-conscious. For example, when we think we are being threatened, our feelings turn defensive and our desire is to fight, freeze, or flee. If the perceived threat is social, we then non-consciously send a message that turns into body language, and that in turn sends a message to others such as: I like it, I hate it, or maybe, I have a better idea.

Just how and when desire turns into decision is impossible to determine. The chances are that it varies by situation. But this we do know: something happens at a certain stage of the mental process whereby our attention passes from desire to action. When mind-bugs are present this handoff can become faulty. *We may not understand our decisions for what they are and, more importantly, what they are not.*

Looked at this way, our mind is continually communicating four kinds of things to us.

Figure 4-1

Our Mind Communicates Four Things

| Meaning of events in our lives |
| Feelings about those events |
| Where to put our energy |
| When and how to take action |

We all have a special relationship with our mental processes that we generally call thinking. The key to improving decisions is to make those non-conscious relationships conscious and deliberate where appropriate.

Exercise

Review Figure 4-1 and the four things our mind communicates. Reflecting on these four functions, identify an example where one of these was in error. For example,

- *Have you ever misinterpreted an event such as the meaning of an email?*
- *Have you ever had a feeling about an interaction with someone else that proved to be erroneous?*
- *Have you ever decided to put energy in an activity and later found it to be a poor choice?*

As humans we all have times when the communications from our mind are faulty. Understanding that this happens to everyone helps us recognize errors in our judgments sooner or even avoid them. On the other hand, if we are quick to defend our thinking even though we have not stopped to examine it, we may unnecessarily make faulty decisions and/or complicate our lives.

ı ı ı ı ı ▪ ▪ ▪ ▬ ▬ ▬ ▬ ▪ ▪ ▪ ı ı ı ı ı

**There are two ways to think,
two ways to feel,
two ways to desire, and
two ways to decide.
We are either mindful of our thinking — or mindless.**

Chapter 5: The Two Ways

People commonly use statistics like a drunken man uses a lamp post: for support rather than illumination.

— *Andrew Lang*

There are two ways to do everything. For example, there are two ways to express your ideas and two ways to listen to ideas of others, two ways to correct and two ways to take correction, two ways to accept help and two ways to help others, two ways to use statistics, and two ways to make any decision.

Figure 5-1

The Two Ways to Do Everything

The Two Ways:	My behavior is:	I am:	Mind-Bugs:
1. I am in command of my thoughts	Reflective	Mindful	Avoided
2. My thoughts are in command of me	Reactive	Mindless	Thrive

Reacting Versus Reflecting

When we are not mindful[50] of our thinking, we *react*[51] to our thoughts, feelings, and desires, without even being aware that we are reacting. Mind-bugs are often a part of our reacting and may lead to biased analyses, behavioral problems, and harmful decisions. We may condemn, criticize, deny, justify, ignore, disengage, blame, and/or defend without full awareness of what we are doing.[52]

One Reaction Sets Off Another

Depending on our initial reaction, we can set off subsequent reactions. For example, if I interpret my manager's performance feedback as an attack, I may be defensive with him. Later I may attack him during a water cooler conversation with a third party. Then I may go home, continue to "carry it with me", reacting again to other innocent bystanders.

Often we live in the second, third, or even tenth generation of our initial reaction, having never understood our reactivity and now are compelled to justify and defend it. The cure is to wake up and accept where we are.** As mindfulness becomes stronger, we become aware earlier and earlier, and eventually we no longer react. We become present with our thoughts and are no longer controlled by them.

Figure 5-2

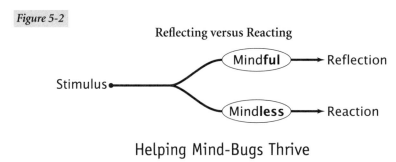

Reflecting versus Reacting

Helping Mind-Bugs Thrive

When we are not in command of our thinking, mind-bugs thrive. They can lead to poor decisions and stimulate dysfunctional organizational be-

---

** "Experiments have shown that in order for a stimulus to reach consciousness, it needs a minimal amount of time to be present, and it needs to have a certain degree of clarity. However, this is not quite enough. The stimulus has to have an interaction with the attention state of the observer. Attention and consciousness are two separate animals." Gazzaniga, Michael S. *Human: the Science behind What Makes Us Unique*. New York: Ecco, 2008. Print.

havior. Figure 5-3 provides a peek at the potential impact to a company's thinking, behavior, and culture.

Figure 5-3

Organizational Thinking and Behavior

Mindless and Reactive My Thoughts are in Command of Me	Mindful and Reflective I am in Command of My Thoughts
Preoccupied	Present
Judgmental	Concerned
Persuading	Educating
Defending	Considering
Justifying	Evaluating
Blaming	Responsible
Arrogant	Humble
Controlling	Empowering
Hypocritical	Sincere
Impatient	Urgent
Suspicious	Observant
Meddling	Helpful
Biased	Impartial
Deceptive	Honest
Self-centered	Fair-minded
Exhausting	Enlivening

Whether or not we are mindful determines whether we reflect or react. Reflecting does not mean we stop *to think*, it means we pause to *think about the quality of our thoughts*: that is, we consider the quality of our thoughts, feelings, and desires before we make decisions. We look for mind-bugs. When we react, our thoughts are in control of us. When we reflect, we are in control of our thinking. Mindfulness gives us power. Mindlessness usually requires us to use force.

Exercise

Here's an exercise to try. Consider any recent decision or behavior by you, another, or a group and reflect on the contrasting pairs of behavioral qualities in Figure 5-3. See if you can identify how mind-bugs might be present. Ponder what kind of internal shift needs to occur for those involved to gain command of their thinking within any pair set. Part of that internal shift requires that we learn to accept that mind-bugs are an inherent part of our thinking, even though we may be unaware of them.

Mind-Bugs Awareness Index

I have developed a simple interactive online tool that helps people increase awareness of the possibility of mind-bugs. It is available for free at http://curecorporatestupidity.com. A manual version appears later in this book. It is a powerful first step to increase awareness that mind-bugs are much more at play than you had believed. It can be a real wake-up call.

ı ı ı ı ı ▪ ▪ ▪ ▪ ▪ ▪ ▪ ▪ ▪ ▪ ▪ ▪ ı ı ı ı ı

**When we think, we learn about the world outside ourselves.
When we think about our thinking,
we learn about the world inside ourselves.
— I call that taking command of our thinking.**

Chapter 6: Taking Command

The chief occupation of mankind is to believe passionately in the not true.

— H.L. Mencken

No one naturally thinks they are not in command of their thoughts. To the contrary, our mind-bugs cause the belief that our thinking is just fine. In this state, we have little desire or motivation to investigate any further. And, we may fear that if we were the first to bring up this possibility at work that others would look down on us. So there you are, the functions of your mind (thoughts, feelings, desires, and decisions) are all wrapped up in a neat package convincing you of the truth. If this is the way you are right now, it is time to *say hello to your mind-bugs*. For the moment, allow yourself to examine this concept without responding to your own bias (and mind-bugs). When the desire to defend your own belief comes up, just recognize your belief for what it is—just one of many options.

Taking Control

When we take command of our thinking, we understand the related roles of thoughts, feelings, desires, and decisions. We recognize that for every feeling we experience, it is connected to thoughts and desires that may non-consciously motivate us to a decision and action. We openly accept that, out of unawareness of flaws in our thoughts, we may react in ways which harm ourselves and others and destroy value in our business.

Mental Breakpoint and Debugging

When we take command, we consciously pay attention to our thoughts. We shine an internal spotlight on them and give them conscious objective mindful examination and assessment.[53] I call this inserting a mental breakpoint. As mentioned earlier, software programmers insert a breakpoint to suspend execution of a program at certain points in order to examine for bugs in the oftentimes millions of lines of code. We can do the same by inserting a mental breakpoint to suspend the process in order to debug our thinking. In doing this, our consciousness is raised and we can identify flaws in our thinking. This turns out to be the "killer app" for improving decisions through taking command of your thinking!

Figure 6-1

Taking Control of Our Thinking Processes

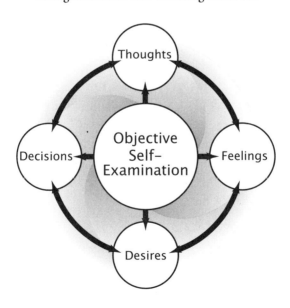

Sounds Simple

In principle, the training of attention to our thoughts seems simple. As you will see, problems arise when thoughts are compulsive and not examined. And when compulsive thoughts are strengthened by such feelings as fear, anger, irritation, apprehension, or craving, our thoughts dominate our attention. They are in command and everything in our conditioning screams,[54] "Hey, look at that! Pay attention to that! Eat that! Drink that! Dislike that!" Without awareness and objective self examination, all the mind can do is repeat the same thought over and over.

Don't Choose to Give Power to a Compulsive Thought

A compulsive thought, whether it is grounded in anger, fear, or a strong desire, does not really have any power of its own. All the power is in the control we non-consciously choose to allow it to have over us. When we understand it for what it is, the thought or desire will be helpless to compel us into action. These mind-bugs are like cockroaches in the kitchen at night—they scatter when the light is turned on.

Making the Shift

Simply put, when we insert a mental breakpoint and objectively examine the elements of our thinking process, we begin to take command of our thinking. We are no longer being controlled by our unexamined thoughts, feelings, desires, and decisions.[55] While the functions are still biologically connected to each other, we intercept them and intentionally look for any that may block seeing the path to good decisions. The simple fact is that there is only one person who stops you from seeing the path—you. Figure 6-2 portrays the shift to being in command of our thinking.

Fig. 6-2

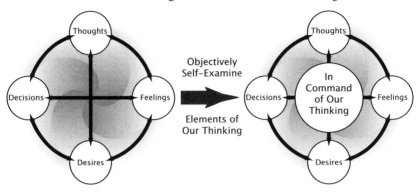

The shift to Being in Command of Our Thinking

The Wisdom of Examining Reality

Nothing can be more important than self awareness of our thoughts, feelings, desires, and decisions. The actions we take are wrapped up in these functions. And, once these have been turned on by our own non-conscious mental reaction, it is difficult to turn them off.

Out of mindlessness we may keep reacting in ways which harm ourselves and others. But when we take command of our thinking our pattern of reacting is interrupted. When we cease to react blindly we are capable of higher quality decisions. We see and understand the real truth. This is the place where we are mindful, where we are reflective, and where we are in command of our thinking. Mindful action can only be positive, creative, and helpful to us and others.

Exercise

Spend some time reflecting as you ask yourself:

- *What important decision have I made that I can now see I made when I was just not in command of my thinking?*
- *What were my thoughts, feelings, and desires at that time?*
- *What impact did they have on my decision?*
- *How would I decide differently now that I can reflect on the situation?*
- *What will I do differently for future decisions?*

In today's world, most people are on such a mental racetrack that they are not present with their decisions. This provides a fertile environment for the growth of mind-bugs. And, as you will see, corporations inherently provide excellent growth conditions for mind-bugs.

۱ ۱ ۱ ۱ ▪ ▪ ■ ■ ▬ ▬ ▬ ▬ ■ ■ ▪ ▪ ۱ ۱ ۱ ۱

It is a sign of "being in command of our thinking" to be able to objectively examine the elements of our thinking process.

What to Remember - Section 1

| | | | | ■ ■ ▬ ▬ ▬ ▬ ■ ■ | | | | |

Most people are not typically conscious of the internal processes they follow to make decisions and take action. When they go astray, bugs in our internal mental processes can cause faulty decisions. I call these mind-bugs.

Our mind communicates four things :

1. Meaning of events in our lives
2. Feelings about those events
3. Where to put our energy
4. When and how to take action

The ancestor of every destructive decision is a fault in one of these. Mind-bugs can exist when our attachment to our thoughts, feelings, desires, and decisions are stronger than our ability to let go of them easily. The result is that we are not in command of our own thinking.

There are two ways to do anything: either we are in command of our thinking, or our thoughts are in command of us. When we objectively examine the elements of our internal processes we insert a mental breakpoint and take command of our thinking. The simple fact is there is only one person who stops you from seeing the path to wisdom—you.

There is a pervasiveness of mind-bugs in corporate decisions—they are hard-wired and highly resistant to feedback, however brutally direct. A decision process free of mind-bugs will ferret out poor quality analysis. The reverse is not true; superb analysis is useless if it contains mind-bugs.

Section 2: Identifying Mind-Bugs

*Naming the mind-bugs allows us to
look for them non-defensively*

▪ ▪ ▪ ▪ ▪ ▪ ▪ ▪ ▪ ▪ ▪ ▪ ▪ ▪ ▪ ▪

Section Contents by Chapter:

8. Meet the Mind-Bugs – Dimensions of Thinking
9. Mind-Bug Reference Guide – 4 Tables, 20 Mind-Bugs
10. The Sufficiency Dimension Mind-Bugs – If You Want More
11. The Accuracy Dimension Mind-Bugs – If You Want More
12. The Beliefs Dimension Mind-Bugs – If You Want More
13. The Social Dimension Mind-Bugs – If You Want More
14. What to Remember

Note to Readers

Our goal is to learn to detect the presence of mind-bugs through a general understanding. This does not require in-depth technical proficiency. Accordingly, if you read through Chapter 8 and "get it", you can skip Chapters 9-12 for now. Circle back when you want to dive down just a little further and get more practical insight.

Chapter 8: Meet the Mind-Bugs

It is not what we don't know that causes problems;
it is what we know that just ain't so.

— Artemus Ward

ı ı ı ı ı ı ∎ ∎ ∎ ∎ ∎ ∎ ∎ ∎ ∎ ∎ ∎ ı ı ı ı ı

This section provides an introduction to the specific mind-bugs I have found occur most often in business decisions. You do not necessarily need to become an expert in the underlying social neuroscience of each one; rather, the key benefit is simply in learning enough to become proficient in recognizing them. This is the first step to avoidance.

Poor Habits of Thinking

Left untrained, we all develop some poor habits of thinking. We are susceptible to making errors in judgment based on distortions in the way we perceive reality. We are all aware that our intuitions can be wrong, but there are cases when we find it difficult to abandon our judgments. Or conversely, we may find that our intuitions and judgments are influenced by unrecognized forces. For example, in business we often find this to be the case because we have specific results that we (or our boss, board of directors, or other stakeholders) *desire* and we attach strong *feelings* to achieving them.

Creating Our Own Problems

We live with the unrealistic but confident sense that we have figured out the way things are, and that we have done that objectively. But mind-bugs may cause self-deception and we can unwittingly become an accomplice in creating our own problems. Here is how I have identified, prioritized, and organized the key mind-bugs as they impact decisions in business.

Figure 8-1

Mind-Bugs and Dimensions

Dimensions			
Sufficiency	Accuracy	Beliefs	Social
Informed Leader Fallacy	Unverified Information vs. Fact	Outcome Attachment	Conforming Error
Source Influence	Generalization without Evidence	Shortcomings Denial	Rose-colored Glasses
Assumption Error	Seeing Patterns that are not real	Closed Mind	Power Insulation
Snap Judgment Defense	Data Rejection	Experience Bias	Status Quo
Shooting the Critics	Data Favoritism	Competency Blindness	Hiding Weakness

Why Do It This Way?

To be useful, the mind-bugs are categorized within four dimensions that are relevant to the elements of reasoning for all decisions. This is not a comprehensive list, but I find it sufficient to apply to a practical method of improving decisions. Some mind-bugs may have other commonly-used descriptors. In that case, I have chosen terminology that I find improves clarity. These are not the only standards that might be used, but are simply what I find to be most useful.

The Four Dimensions

Business decisions are generally based on verified information communicated from a point of view within a social context. In general, *Sufficiency and Accuracy* are concerned with quality control of inputs, those pieces of information we use to make decisions. When we look for mind-bugs in these dimensions we are performing a quality control check that our inputs are both accurate and sufficient. *Beliefs* address how we personally color the decision process with our own perspective, desires, values, and feelings. *Social* considers the influence of other people, groups, power structure, bureaucracy, and vested interest.

Figure 8-2

The Four Dimensions of Mind-Bugs

Dimensions			
Sufficiency	Accuracy	Beliefs	Social
Mind-Bugs in these dimensions lead to errors in the way we gather information		Mind-Bugs in these dimensions lead to errors in the way we process information	
Do I have the correct inputs?	Are the inputs truthful?	How do I color my decision process?	What is the influence of others?

The Gathering and Processing Dilemma

The way we gather information affects what we process and the way we process information affects what we gather. Mind-bugs cause flaws in these fundamental decision-making activities and have an impact across the four dimensions. Making the best decisions requires that we take command of our internal mental processes in each dimension. When we do, we are taking command of our thinking. Most of the time we are not conscious of our thoughts, feelings, desires, and decisions in each of these dimensions as we make decisions in business and in life.

Avoiding mind-bugs is not a new process to add on top of everything else; rather, it is the way we go about all we do.

Chapter 9:
Mind-Bug Reference Guide

Not everything is as we see it to be.

I I I I I ▪ ■ ■ ■ ■ ■ ■ ■ ■ ■ ■ ■ ■ I I I I I

    The following four tables in this chapter provide a summary of the key mind-bugs found in each of the four dimensions. The tables are followed by four chapters with more comprehensive explanations. You can decide to read the comprehensive explanations now or later depending on your need and mood. Once you have reviewed the four tables in this chapter, consider the exercise that follows them.

Table 9-1

The Sufficiency Dimension Mind-Bugs	
The requirement to make decisions based on both relevant and significant information of adequate breadth and depth.	
Informed Leader Fallacy	A belief by a leader that he/she is better informed and has better instincts than others, simply because he/she is the leader.
Example:	A high level manager decides to fire an employee without seeking the advice of others because he believes he is well-informed. After the fact, he learns things about the employee's performance that indicate his was a poor decision.
Source Influence	Determining level of sufficiency depending on the source.
Example:	When our boss suggests something, we may subconsciously accept it as complete without any challenge. When someone we are competing with suggests something, we may seek to find fault.
Assumption Error	Basing decisions on assumptions we believe are true, without challenging those assumptions.
Example:	A CEO assumes his company can design a component better than purchasing an existing component from outside the company. Result, spending money on R&D when a good solution already exists.
Snap Judgment Defense	Defending decisions made solely on snap judgment.
Example:	Due to the high pressure atmosphere at work, a manager makes a snap judgment to move an employee from one position to another and informs the employee of the change. When another manager questions this move, the decision-maker becomes defensive and incapable of hearing another perspective.
Shooting the Critics	The tendency to marginalize people who disagree with us.
Example:	The head of quality at a large manufacturer hires an employee who comes with new ideas and a desire to express them. Sometimes this employee disagrees with his boss. Over time, the boss quits inviting him to key meetings and eventually he is completely out of the decision loop.

Table 9-2

The Accuracy Dimension Mind-Bugs	
The requirement to make decisions based on information that is clearly defined, reliable, factual, precise, and fair.	
Unverified Information vs. Fact	Causes us to confuse unverified information with facts.
Example: I want to drop the price of our product A to generate more sales this month. I trust that three of my experienced colleagues believe that doing this is a good idea (unverified information). However, a customer survey would provide facts that show customer inventory is already too high and no sales increase would occur (fact). If I fail to examine my mind-bugs, I will drop prices on unverified information, rather than fact.	
Generalization without Evidence	Making generalizations without the evidence to back them up.
Example: The profit margin on product A has maintained a steady 35% for two years. Is that sufficient to project that margin will be 35% for the next five years? No, not based solely on this information.	
Seeing Patterns that are not Real	Seeing patterns in random data when none exist.
Example: Since customers have not complained about the quality of our new product we must not have any problems.	
Data Rejection	A reflex-like rejection of new facts because they contradict existing norms.
Example: A Fortune 500 company appointed its public relations department to organize all the divisional websites to harmonize with the corporate site. Businesses with different needs had their sites rejected without consideration—chaos broke out.	
Data Favoritism	Selecting, using, and favoring data in a self-serving, unquestioning way.
Example: One study suggests that Product A performs at 2 ounces per gallon. Another study, of equal quality, concludes that Product A performs at 5 ounces per gallon. I want to beat competition, so I use the data from the first survey without determining why differing results occurred.	

Table 9-3

The Beliefs Dimension Mind-Bugs	
The requirement to consider the influence of one's own perspective, desires, values, and emotions in conjunction with any decision.	
Outcome Attachment	Being so attached to outcomes that serve our interest that we fail to look for problems in our thinking and decisions.
Example: A CEO knows that her job depends on hitting next year's numbers. When there is an opportunity to sandbag revenue from this year and put it into next year, she decides to do it without examining the consequences.	
Shortcomings Denial	Underestimating our own shortcomings by not knowing or believing we have them or rationalizing and assuming we can control them.
Example: When Bob receives a promotion to Director of Sales, his boss suggests he hire an assistant to help pay attention to the details. Bob knows that he is not a detail person, but decides against the assistant. He believes that because he is aware of his shortcoming he will overcome it.	
Closed Mind	The inability to hold and examine two opposing views at the same time and to be closed to other perspectives than our own.
Example: I am convinced that the new product we have been investing in for the last 18 months will be successful. When our head of marketing expresses concerns about the product, I pay lip service to her concerns and then continue with the product launch, as is.	
Experience Bias	Believing that future events will occur in a specific way, based on prior experience—not realizing that past experience is not always predictive of future reality.
Example: If I have lead a successful product launch in the past I may believe that the conditions and decisions of the next product launch will be similar. If my belief is strong I fail to look for contradictory evidence and make a higher-risk decision.	
Competency Blindness	Believing others are competent in areas when they are not and vice versa when it suits our subconscious needs.
Example: My right-hand person has always delivered. No matter what I have asked him to do, he has taken on the challenge and come through with flying colors. I decide to have him tackle a problem we are having with quality control. He fails miserably. I did not consider whether he was competent in that particular expertise.	

Table 9-4

The Social Dimension Mind-Bugs
Consideration of the influence of the group's definition of reality along with bureaucracy, power structure, and vested interests, in conjunction with decisions.

Conforming Error	Subconsciously conforming our thinking to the thinking of our group.

Example: When Bob first joined the company, he couldn't believe the inefficiencies that existed in the billing process. But, everyone said that this is just the way things are in their industry. Over time, Bob has come to believe them.

Rose-colored Glasses	Overestimating the likelihood of positive events because everyone in the group believes they will happen.

Example: A special task force has been in place for the launch of a new product. They have worked hard for the past six months to get the product to market. They feel so good about the product that they promise a certain level of revenue in the first year without data to back up their projections.

Power Insulation	The power structure of a group discourages disturbances to their beliefs.

Example: A consultant is brought in to help a group with strategic planning. He quickly realizes that they are not achieving the kind of margins that are possible. When he challenges them, he is told that he simply doesn't understand because their business is different. The management team refuses to objectively evaluate his recommendations.

Status Quo	Sticking to the status quo and creating significant friction that works against new ideas.

Example: Your company is considering introducing digital machinery on the shop floor. Several foremen point out the many ways that the learning curve will seriously slow down current production and quality, ignoring the large benefits of increased quality and production once the transition period is over.

Hiding Weaknesses	The tendency to hide our weaknesses by presenting the most favorable picture to outsiders.

Example: A partner company is brought in to develop software that will analyze project management efficiency. The partner is not told up front that there is deep internal disagreement as to the accuracy of the data on which the software will be based.

Exercise

Identify an important decision you will be making over the next 30 days or so and write it down. It can be in your business or personal life. Review the four dimensions of mind-bugs in relationship to your decision. Answer the following questions:

1. *Assuming the decision goes well, how will I have avoided each mind-bug?*
2. *Assuming the decision does not go well, how might each mind-bug have negatively impacted the decision?*

Share this exercise with the group involved in this decision and execution. The odds of avoiding mind-bugs in a group setting increases when discussion of them is widespread.

**Not everything that counts can be counted.
And not everything that can be counted, counts.**

— *Albert Einstein*

The Sufficiency Dimension Mind-Bugs

Not everything we view as sufficient, is.

ı ı ı ı ı ı ■ ■ ■ ■ ■ ■ ■ ■ ■ ı ı ı ı ı

Sufficiency Dimension – The requirement to make decisions based on both relevant and significant information of adequate breadth and depth.

The sufficiency dimension addresses the mind-bugs in business that cause us to believe that an argument and its support are sufficient when there are actually gaps. This is particularly true if we have a vested interest or personal belief, or there is a group dynamic involved. We may present and/or accept data as sufficient for a decision that does not completely frame the situation in a balanced fashion as long as it supports the decision we subconsciously want to make.

Sufficiency Mind-Bug #1 — Informed Leader Fallacy

We deeply want to be led by people who know what they're doing and who don't have to think about it too much. So by the time we achieve a leadership position ourselves, we are good at making others feel positive in our judgment, even if there's no strong basis. But the amount of success it takes for leaders to become overconfident isn't terribly large. Some achieve a reputation for great successes when in fact all they have done is take chances that happened to work out. The fierce personal confidence and sense of infallibility that characterizes many leaders serves as a breeding ground for this mind-bug. Most decision makers will trust their own intuitions because they think they see the situation clearly. Accordingly, it causes leaders to fall into a trap of believing they are better informed than they really are. Everything is based on the appearance of being informed, rather than actual information. How long do you think that success will last if this mind-bug bites you?

Sufficiency Mind-Bug #2 — Source Influence

This mind-bug affects the conditions and inputs we accept as sufficient. For example, when our boss suggests something we may non-consciously accept it as complete without any challenge because our boss is the source. It may be that we fear having a conflict by proposing an alternative to his thinking.

If our company acquires another company, we may arbitrarily decide that our way is better than theirs without sufficiently mindful consideration. So we non-consciously go about gathering information under the influence of the source and create an environment for faulty decisions. And if decisions do not go well, we find comfort that we can always blame our boss later.

Sufficiency Mind-Bug #3 — Assumptions Error

Assumptions always underlie decisions and are something we often take for granted or presuppose. Usually it is something we do not question and has become part of our system of beliefs.[56] When this mind-bug is active, we believe our assumptions are true and do not challenge them. Or, the challenge is self-justifying lip service. If our belief is not sound, our assumption is not sound, and hence unjustified. The key point is that we all make many assumptions as we go about our daily life and we ought to be able to recognize and question them. This mind-bug gets in the way and causes us to make decisions based on faulty assumptions. Furthermore, we spend more time seeking to justify and defend our assumptions than to examine them objectively.

Sufficiency Mind-Bug #4 — Snap Judgment Defense

Due to the hard-wired threat response in our brain, we make rapid judgments about what's happening which allows us to quickly determine what information is most relevant—and take speedy action. Otherwise, we get into an information overload mode.[57] Rather than seeking confirmation, we use past experience to guide us. This is helpful when the threat is physical and we must act without delay. But in business, we often find it easy to lose track of how quickly we are judging a situation or how much we've explained away. Since we associate leadership with decisiveness, being decisive becomes a self-driven attribute. That pushes us to make decisions fairly quickly for fear of being seen as unable to make up our mind. Once triggered, this mind-bug shifts into defense or fight mode, causing us (the afflicted) to focus solely on explaining and defending our snap judgment. Our logic circuits shut down and we are unable to objectively consider points of view that conflict with our own.[58] We may act like we are listening, but we are only giving it lip service—and most everyone knows it but us.

Sufficiency Mind-Bug #5 — Shooting the Critics

Leaders know that any decision they make is subject to their judgment being questioned. And whether they're fully aware of it or not, they're really not in the market to have their decisions, beliefs, and choices questioned.[59] Whether we are team leaders or CEOs, we subconsciously develop the tendency to marginalize people who disagree with us. When this happens people stop telling the truth. They avoid rocking the boat and just quietly stay out of the line of fire. This mind-bug causes intolerance for challenge and acceptance of our beliefs as sufficient, leaving huge gaps in mindful evaluation and judgments.

Exercise

Identify a decision you will be making over the next 30 days or so and write it down. It can be in your business or personal life. Review the Sufficiency mind-bugs in relationship to each decision. Answer the following questions:

1. Assuming the decision goes well, how will I have avoided each **Sufficiency** *mind-bug?*

2. *Assuming the decision does not go well, how might each* **Sufficiency** *mind-bug have negatively impacted the decision?*

Share this exercise with the group involved in this decision and execution. The odds of avoiding mind-bugs in a group setting increases when they are regularly and openly discussed.

**It is not our thoughts themselves that create risk—
It is our attachment to them as being sufficient.**

The Accuracy Dimension Mind-Bugs

Not everything presented as accurate, is.

▪ ▪ ▪ ▪ ▪ ▪ ▪ ▪ ▪ ▪ ▪ ▪ ▪ ▪ ▪ ▪ ▪ ▪ ▪

Accuracy Dimension – The requirement to make decisions based on clearly defined, reliable, factual, precise, and fair information.

The accuracy dimension is one of the underpinnings of any decision. If inputs are not accurate then decisions will be faulty regardless of the quality of the ensuing decision-making process. As you will see, these mind-bugs feed off each other and when one is present, the others are lurking nearby.

Accuracy Mind-Bug #1 — Unverified Information vs Fact

This mind-bug causes a failure to appreciate the difference between unverified information and fact. All facts are information, but not all information is fact. Facts are verifiably true and real. They are the raw data, the actual observations. This failure is not intentional but rather the misrepresentation of fact is committed subconsciously in a way we cannot sense.[60] What we do sense is a feeling of satisfaction that prevents any objective analysis on our part. This is not comprehensible to any outside observer and when the individual is one of power or popularity, or the decision is already favored, the information goes without a fair-minded challenge and evaluation. In this case, people are not even trying to be objective or to learn about themselves. Many times they are reacting to their desire to prolong the status quo or achieve personal gains, and allowing that to influence the way they gather information.

Accuracy Mind-Bug #2 — Generalization without Evidence

Generalizations can be a valid method of argument when they are based on sound conclusions from repeated experiences or observations. This mind-bug causes faulty conclusions because:

- there is a lack of a sufficient number of instances to draw a conclusion
- the conclusion is not consistent with the evidence

We frequently are infected by this mind-bug when we have a vested interest and emotional attachment. This causes us to naturally tend to believe our thoughts are accurate because they are ours, and therefore the thoughts of those who disagree are wrong. For example, if the profit margin on Product A has been a steady 35% for two years, is that sufficient to project they will be 35% for the next five years, and thus we should choose to increase our investment? No, not based solely on this information; this is a generalization without evidence.

Accuracy Mind-Bug #3 — Seeing Patterns That Are Not Real

Pattern recognition is important to making decisions. This mind-bug causes the afflicted to see and believe in patterns or connections in random or meaningless data when none exist. We believe in the apparition and our faith is generally driven by our unevaluated desires to have circumstances be as we want them to be. Since pattern recognition may be related to plans and goals, it may be a matter of group beliefs rather than solitary delusion. For example, when just a few potential customers give us feedback that supports our business desires, we may be seduced into reading more into the feedback than exists. Then coupled with mind-bug #1, we present our conclusions as facts when they are not. If the group shares the same desire and mind-bug, the myth is perpetuated as fact.

Accuracy Mind-Bug #4 — Data Rejection

Have you ever rejected some data that might conflict with a decision? This mind-bug causes a failure to appreciate that we may reject new facts because they contradict entrenched rules and norms. There is intense pressure to produce at work, and to produce high-impact results. When we non-consciously choose to reject data that conflicts with "how we do things" we naturally defend our point of view. And, we may react to questions as a personal attack; if so, then look out for the "brain hijack". The result is that this mind-bug causes us to use data in a self-serving manner and blinds us to anything different. If questioned, we may feign ignorance and blame the first author or data generator for any ambiguities. This devious behavior is a mind-bug at work.

Accuracy Mind-Bug #5 — Data Favoritism

When afflicted by this mind-bug it is as if we are a data racist. In this case it is not an issue as to whether the data was created equally; it is that we select and use what we want. For example, if two equal quality studies produced different results, we tend to rely on the data that supports our position. This may seem elementary, but most of the time if data supports our desires we naturally tend to accept it. If data doesn't support our position, we tend to examine it more critically. We are not aware that we are playing favorites with data and are self-deceived.

Exercise

Identify a decision you will be making over the next 30 days or so and write it down. It can be in your business or personal life. Review the Accuracy mind-bugs in relationship to each decision. Answer the following questions:

1. *Assuming the decision goes well, how will I have avoided each* **Accuracy** *mind-bug?*
2. *Assuming the decision does not go well, how might each* **Accuracy** *mind-bug have negatively impacted the decision?*

Share this exercise with the group involved in this decision and execution. The odds of avoiding mind-bugs in a group setting increases when discussion of them is widespread.

**It is not our thoughts themselves that create risk—
It is our attachment to them as being accurate.**

The Beliefs Dimension Mind-Bugs

Just because we believe something doesn't make it true.

Beliefs Dimension – The requirement to consider the influence of one's own point of view, desires, values, principles, and emotional connections in conjunction with any decision.

The beliefs dimension addresses the idea that whenever we reason, we do that within a point of view. Any flaw in that point of view is a possible source of faulty thinking and mind-bugs. Our point of view is influenced by our feelings, desires, thoughts, and decisions. Belief mind-bugs may cause us to unknowingly draw conclusions and make decisions based on limited, unfair, and misleading personal interpretations of information. We can get so locked in that we are unable to see the issue from other rational points of view. Belief mind-bugs are so strong that they can cause us to corrupt the noblest virtues and justify it to ourselves. An example is how we might corrupt the truth.

> ### How Mind-Bugs Corrupt the Truth
> It is true because:
>   a. I believe it.
>   b. I want to believe it.
>   c. I have always believed it.
>   d. It is in my best interest for it to be true.

With these corruptions, we can justify anything to ourselves. You will not need to look long or deeply at religion, politics, and organizations to find many examples of belief mind-bugs going unchallenged and wreaking havoc.

Beliefs Mind-Bug #1 — Outcome Attachment

Non-consciously we are all attached to outcomes that serve our interests, helping us get what we want or what we believe others expect of us. When this mind-bug strikes, the attachment is so strong that we may be willing to manipulate numbers in order to hit quotas, or declare a mission accomplished when in fact it isn't.[61] It seriously affects how we gather information so that we search in a way that supports the outcome to which we are attached. As stated earlier, the way we process information affects what we gather and the way we gather information affects how we process it. It is a debilitating problem when it affects how we make decisions. Our feelings and emotional reactions tend to validate our thinking while we seek to justify our thoughts, feelings, desires, and decisions. We are confident in the truth of our own belief system, however flawed.[62]

Beliefs Mind-Bug #2 — Shortcoming Denial

We all have shortcomings that we don't realize can contribute to poor decisions. This mind-bug evolves in phases. At first we don't *know* we have a shortcoming; we are unskilled and unaware. In the next phase we don't *believe* we have a shortcoming; rather than being unaware, we are unskilled and in disbelief. Then we *rationalize* and *minimize* the shortcoming, making the critical assumption that it is not affecting any critical decision. Later we think we can *control* the problem, and at times we believe the shortcoming has been addressed or just gone away. All these are ways we stay in various levels of denial of our shortcomings and belief in our judgment. And in denial, we exist in a distorted reality, afflicted with a mind-bug that may cause faulty thinking and poor quality decisions. So, it would be wise to never underestimate the non-conscious power of Shortcoming Denial; it is a very potent mind-bug.

Beliefs Mind-Bug #3 — Closed Mind

When we are afflicted with this mind-bug we subconsciously shut down the very thing that can help us examine our own beliefs: mindful evaluation of diversity of thought. In essence, things are the way I see them because that is the way I see it. As perpetrators, we are sometimes not aware of doing this. Other times we may even be proud of it. We make the self-serving assumption that we have figured out the way things are and anything that challenges our point of view becomes "unthinkable". It is not that we shoot the critics or fail to listen. To the contrary, we may spend time demonstrating our listening skills to others to prove we are good listeners, but afflicted as we are, we just don't hear them. We simply are not aware that we don't allow ourselves to hold and mindfully examine two opposing views at the same time. We give lots of lip service to ourselves and others, but true diversity of thought is shut down. Once infected, we feel pretty good until the day of reckoning, when we ask ourselves: "What was I thinking when I made THAT decision?"[63]

Beliefs Mind-Bug #4 — Experience Bias

It is logical to consider experience. This mind-bug afflicts us with the tendency to believe that events will occur in a specific way based on prior experiences. Our exclusive focus misses that human reasoning is accompanied by various subjective experiences, including our interpretation of our thoughts feelings, desires, and decisions. This has an affect on our recall and objective comparison.[64] Once afflicted, our belief is so strong that we fail to look for contradictory evidence and impute hostile motives to even the most helpful folks who question the relevance of our experience.

Beliefs Mind-Bug #5 — Competency Blindness

Companies naturally seek relevant expertise. This mind-bug affects how we perceive the level of competence in others that may provide useful advice, recommendations, and decisions. Those afflicted may believe others are competent in areas when they are not and vice versa. This may be driven by our desire to justify an Outcome Attachment mind-bug. Once afflicted we are not aware of our blindness and can trust the wrong parties, while overlooking and disrespecting those with wisdom in an area. In this case we are blind to the competency gap and blind to the fact that we are blind. Accordingly, we are not in denial; rather, we portray our belief to others with convincing but unknowingly hollow examples and references. We live in peace with our belief unless challenged by others or until the fateful day when false competency is debunked by a critical failed decision. Of course, then we can blame those we inappropriately trusted.

Exercise

Identify a decision you will be making over the next 30 days or so and write it down. It can be in your business or personal life. Review the Beliefs mind-bugs in relationship to each decision. Answer the following questions:

1. *Assuming the decision goes well, how will I have avoided each* **Beliefs** *mind-bug?*
2. *Assuming the decision does not go well, how might each* **Beliefs** *mind-bug have negatively impacted the decision?*

Share this exercise with the group involved in this decision and execution. The odds of avoiding mind-bugs in a group setting increases when they are openly and regularly discussed.

**It is not our beliefs themselves that create risk—
It is our attachment to them as being correct.**

The Social Dimension Mind-Bugs

One man alone can be pretty stupid, but for real high performance stupidity nothing beats teamwork.

— *Edward Abbey*

Social Dimension – The requirement to consider the influence of the group's definition of reality, as well as bureaucracy, power structure, and vested interests in conjunction with any decisions.

Living a human life entails a variety of relationships and membership in an assortment of groups. Both the interaction and the groups influence our thoughts, feelings, desires, and decisions. Every organization consists not only of individuals, but a hierarchy of power among those individuals. No matter how noble the group's goal, there is often a struggle for power beneath the surface. Personal strategies may be obscure and not apparent even to those who are using them.

Social Mind-Bug #1 — Conforming Error

Groups of people generally have a reason for existence. This mind-bug causes us to conform to the thinking of our group. Once "brain washed" we are of little value in providing constructive challenges to the group's norms and merely act as an echo chamber reinforcing the group's beliefs, however misguided. Like Groupthink,[65] Conforming Error is a type of thought within a deeply cohesive group whose members try to minimize conflict and reach consensus without critically testing, analyzing, and evaluating ideas.

Social Mind-Bug #2 — Rose-Colored Glasses

Some people are naturally optimistic. This mind-bug causes people in groups to overestimate the likelihood of positive events. In essence their truth is corrupted by: "It will happen this way because we believe it will happen this way". Many other mind-bugs contribute to and reinforce this one, including: The Informed Leader Fallacy, Experience Bias, Emotional Attachments, and Shortcomings Denial. The result is the growth of other mind-bugs that corrupt both the gathering of inputs of our decisions as well as the decision process itself. Living with the false reality created by this mind-bug causes people and teams to tend to over-commit and under-deliver. Then they look to justify and blame rather than accept responsibility. If the infected leader is powerful, charismatic, and popular, the risk of damage can be significant when he is under the influence of this mind-bug.[66]

Social Mind-Bug #3 — Power Insulation

All companies and organizations have a structure. This mind-bug causes the power structure of any group to unknowingly fail to welcome disturbances to the group's beliefs, along with the beliefs of the power structure within the group. When asked, an afflicted power structure will respond in denial: "we get it, but we aren't like that. That won't affect us". When different points of view are interpreted as disturbances, the very power structure designed and empowered to serve the organization becomes a constraint that stifles operations. Rather than focusing on serving customers, the organization now is focused on serving the power structure. Insulated from reality and truth, information is served up with unrecognized distortions and decision quality suffers.

Social Mind-Bug #4 — Status Quo

Most decisions have a status quo alternative, defined as doing nothing or maintaining our current or previous decision. This mind-bug causes us to disproportionately stick with the status quo and creates significant friction that works against the momentum and traction of new ideas, thinking, and options.[67] New evidence that contradicts the status quo is cleverly rejected through the infection of other mind-bugs. Defense mechanisms are triggered and emotions can reach dysfunctional proportions. When the Status Quo mind-bug is deeply entrenched, corporations are at significant risk of being displaced by new technology and novel business models. The business landscape is littered with the bankruptcy remains of those companies. When corporations are trying to change and individuals are creating friction, their jobs and careers are at risk and life can be very stressful for everyone involved.

Social Mind-Bug #5 — Hiding Weakness

Just like an injured animal, this mind-bug causes individuals, teams, departments, and corporations to non-consciously hide their weaknesses. It is based on fear. Unaware, they are driven to present the most favorable picture to those outside the group. "Don't air our dirty laundry in public" becomes the unspoken operating principle, resulting in the development of "silos" within organizations. Ironically, this leads to greater weakness, as permanent improvement is a challenge under the shroud of secrecy. Every person and organization has weaknesses. This mind-bug prevents us from seeing and addressing them effectively. Even when we do air weaknesses, we subconsciously present them in the most favorable light.

Exercise

Identify a decision you will be making over the next 30 days or so and write it down. It can be in your business or personal life. Review the Social mind-bugs in relationship to each decision. Answer the following questions:

1. *Assuming the decision goes well, how will I have avoided each* **Social** *mind-bug?*
2. *Assuming the decision does not go well, how might each* **Social** *mind-bug have negatively impacted the decision?*

Share this exercise with the group involved in this decision and execution. The odds of avoiding mind-bugs in a group setting increases when they are openly and regularly discussed.

| | | | | | | | | | | | | | | | | | | | | |

Superiority in power does not equal superiority in thinking.

Chapter 14:
What to Remember - Section 2

To be useful, the mind-bugs are categorized within four dimensions that are relevant to the elements of reasoning for all decisions. We take command of our internal mental processes in each dimension for best decision making. When we do, we take command of our thinking.

Most of the time we are not conscious of our thoughts, feelings, desires, and decisions in each of these dimensions as we make decisions in business and in life.

Dimensions, Mind-Bugs, and Definitions		
Sufficiency	Informed Leader Fallacy	A belief by a leader that he/she is better informed and has better instincts than others, simply because he/she is the leader.
	Source Influence	Determining level of sufficiency depending on the source.
	Assumption Error	Basing decisions on assumptions we believe are true, without challenging those assumptions.
	Snap Judgment Defense	Defending decisions made on solely on snap judgment.
	Shooting the Critics	The tendency to marginalize people who disagree with us.
Accuracy	Unverified Information vs Fact	Causes us to confuse unverified information with facts.
	Generalization without Evidence	Making generalizations without the evidence to back them up.
	Seeing Patterns that are not Real	Seeing patterns in random data when none exist.
	Data Rejection	A reflex-like rejection of new facts because they contradict existing norms.
	Data Favoritism	Selecting, using, and favoring data in a self-serving, unquestioning way.
Beliefs	Outcome Attachment	Being so attached to outcomes that serve our interest that we fail to look for problems in our thinking and decisions.
	Shortcomings Denial	Underestimating our own shortcomings by not believing we have them and rationalizing and assuming we can control them.
	Closed Mind	The inability to hold and examine two opposing views at the same time and to be closed to other perspectives than ours.
	Experience Bias	Believing that future events will occur in a specific way based on our prior experience, and not seeing how conditions differ.
	Competency Blindness	Believing others are competent in areas when they are not and vice versa when it suits our subconscious needs.
Social	Conforming Error	Subconsciously conforming our thinking to the thinking of our group.
	Rose Colored Glasses	Overestimating the likelihood of positive events because everyone in the group believes they will happen.
	Power Insulation	The power structure discourages disturbances to group beliefs.
	Status Quo	Sticking to the status quo and creating significant friction that works against new ideas.
	Hiding Weaknesses	The tendency to hide our weaknesses by presenting the most favorable picture to outsiders.

Section 3: Avoiding Mind-Bugs

Introducing the Concepts, Tools, and Practices

Section Contents by Chapter:

15. Defining the Problem – Thinking Gone Awry
16. The Solution – 6 Step Path to Better Decisions
17. Step 1 – Improving My Own Thinking
18. Moving from Step 1 to Step 2 – The Two Questions
19. Step 2 – Improving Interaction in Groups
20. Step 2 - Cont. – The Two Ways of Interacting with Others
21. Step 3 – Improving Learning and Feedback
22. Step 4 – Decisions and The 30 Second Decision Scan
23. Step 4 - Cont. – The Debugging Process
24. Step 5 – Correction
25. Step 6 – Using the Path to Better Decisions
26. What Prevents the First Step? – Getting Off to the Right Start
27. The Age of Quality Thinking – Thought Governance

Note to Readers

There are many ways to use this book. You are about to learn some tools and practices. You do not have to do them all right away to get benefit. Just reading the book will expand your thinking. But growth for you and your organization depends on putting your learning into practice. Perhaps you have an issue where better quality thinking will be helpful. Select a practice and start there. I sense you will be glad you did.

Chapter 15: Defining the Problem

Many of humankind's greatest disasters have been the result of thinking gone awry.

— Barry F. Anderson

Mind-bugs are like bugs in computer software but they affect our mental processes. They make thinking go awry. As a product of human nature, they are hard-wired and highly resistant to feedback. Mind-bugs can exist when our attachment to our thoughts, feelings, desires, and decisions are stronger than our ability to let go of them. And in reality, most of us are simply unaware of our mind-bugs.

Corporations are Predisposed to Mind-Bugs

Almost nowhere are people more attached to thoughts of goals, objectives, targets, and outcomes than in the world of corporations. When making decisions in business we do that only in the context of achieving specific results. They are drilled into our heads and become automatic thoughts: hit our objectives, make our numbers, be a team player, stand out from the crowd, receive a bonus, get promoted, or live in fear that you won't have a job. And as you have read, fear is an extremely powerful motivator.[68] It is an unfortunate dichotomy that the rigid attention on outcomes that is required for alignment and execution may hinder achieving them in the big picture.[69] The contradiction is that while leaders want employees "focused like a laser beam", preoccupation with outcomes can render them extremely susceptible to mind-bugs.

Hiding in the Least Expected Places

Indeed, detecting mind-bugs presents a challenge because of their resemblance to operating styles that have served both employees and their managers seemingly well. Examples include: "selecting" information to sell a project to the next level of decision makers, identifying patterns in data to justify a point of view, seeking consensus and alignment in meetings, not "rocking the boat" with your boss, becoming adept at defending decisions regardless of the outcome, being seen as a team player, and honoring the power structure. Most of us have experienced automatic and mindless states. For example, if we drive the same route to work daily, it is likely we are thinking about many other things and the driving happens automatically without conscious thought unless a driving problem surfaces. In a sense, we have over-learned these routines, and left unchallenged they can become hiding places for mind-bugs. It is insufficient to "just let go" considering that we may not be aware of how "attached" we really are or how much we are caught up in habitual patterns of thinking.[70]

The Role of Fear

As we learned in Section One, a hard-wired response is triggered in the brain when it perceives a threat. The most relevant threat in business is anything that causes the brain to trigger fear. Natural selection has resulted in the development of social fears, which abound on the job. They include those related to loss, rejection, failure, self image, status, and personal security.[71] The part of the brain involved, the amygdala, governs feelings, impulses, drives, and instinctive action.[72] This brings our body into the story, since we feel with our bodies, and our brain is always influenced by how our body is feeling.[73]

Non-conscious and Automatic

Because the response to social fear is automatic and faster than re-flective action, fear limits our ability to think. Much of our behavior in social life is an automatic state with rigid biases and predetermined rules, and operates quite independently of conscious control.†† While automatic behavior is desirable in many situations, it can limit our ability to think rationally about a decision that has already been constructed in our mind. For example, it's far easier stating a commitment and then putting it off, than actually working through the fear of disappointing a boss or colleague by not committing to what they desire. Without intervention, mind-bugs thrive and the risk of disappointing results and self-inflicted problems increases.

Human Capacity Limits

The general consensus is that the maximum number of bits of infor-mation the average person can keep in our working memory at one time is approximately seven.[74] One credible study even has it that the number of truly independent thoughts we can entertain at one time is actually closer to three.[75] But the maximum number of thoughts we can think at once is approximately one.‡‡ That means we are regularly operating in excess of our available working memory capacity at work. Indeed, even when we have the sense that we might be thinking two things at once, careful intro-spection usually reveals that we are either having a single thought about a category of things ("All the parts of this project seem to be on schedule") or that we rapidly move back and forth between two thoughts ("The proj-ect is on schedule—but the cost is over budget"). The effort required and sequential nature of reflective thinking makes it fragile: even a small, mo-

---

†† Scientists call this automaticity. "People have unconscious automatic responses to things their mind likes or dislikes, from food or books to ideas and social groups. When we do not have the time, inclination, or the ability to study or consciously correct these reactions we are behaving on 'autopilot.'" Wheatley, T., and D. M. Wegner. "Automaticity of Action, Psychology of." *International Encyclopedia of the Social & Behavioral Sciences* (2001): 991-93. Print.

‡‡ "Alas, if there is one clear fact about reflective consciousness, it is that it comes and goes. Like the refrigerator light, reflective consciousness is always on when we check it; but like the refrigerator light, it is probably off more often than on (Schooler, in press)." Lieberman, M., R. Gaunt, D. Gilbert, and Y. Trope. "Reflexion and Reflection: A Social Cognitive Neuroscience Approach to Attributional Inference." *Advances in Experimental Social Psychology* 34 (2002): 199-249. Print.

mentary distraction can derail reflective thinking and allow mind-bugs to exist in our decisions.

Predicting Mind-Bugs

While companies spend considerable energy reporting on and explaining the past, they also try to predict the future all the time. Quarterly, annual, and long range financial forecasts, estimates of future supply and demand, and predictions of competitive response are but a few of the cases. While there are many variables that are considered in these exercises, seldom do they include a consideration of human mental processes. And much of the time that is where bugs occur. The problem is us. We predict the future and analyze the past while spending insufficient time in the present, the only place we can make a difference—and, the only place we can eliminate mind-bugs before they bite us.

No Psychic Hot Lines

My research has lead to the realization that, as humans, we are dreadful at understanding our own patterns of thinking and their effect on decision making.[76] *And yet, most corporate projections assume an ideal decision maker, one who is fully informed and completely rational.* It is no wonder that we spend more time fixing problems that go wrong than helping them go right.[77] I am not suggesting dialing a psychic hot line, although that is what some companies might as well do when they overlook the potential impact of mind-bugs.

The Brain Acts without Thinking

The brain is a biological organ. In simplified terms, one major process of the brain is automation: to produce action without thinking. To achieve this noble purpose it develops subconscious hard-wired circuits that produce a range of activities such as executing the biological processes that keep us alive, quickly reacting to threats with the "fight or flight response," or reading sheet music and automatically hitting the correct key on a piano. For this role, the brain operates on the essential principle of "mindlessness." Like computers, reducing response time is a priority. Your automated brain couldn't care less what you think.

The Mind's Job is to Create Thought

In very basic terms, our mind is our individual personal experience of the world. Different than our brain, our mind is focused on making meaning of events in our lives and deciding where to put our energy. Going about its job, it assigns feelings and desires to events and decisions. These events trigger a stimulus causing our mind to react and continuously serve up thoughts. For survival, the processes of the brain take priority over those of the mind, resulting in unexamined thoughts, feelings, desires, and decisions. Over time, the consequence can be an accumulation of faulty beliefs, biased judgments, and compulsive habits of thinking.

The Brain and Mind – An Example

Suppose that you are singled out to be responsible for developing a new business endeavor for your company after substantial internal competition for the role. You believe that by choosing you as the development leader, the company has tremendous trust in your ability, even though the business area is new to the company. After substantial research you are certain you know what is required to make the decision and definitely understand more about the project than anyone in the organization. Your belief is strong that the investment would be a good one and that it would be a big boost to your career as well.

Finally, you present your recommendation to the review board to seek approval. As you expected, the questions naturally begin and you are ready to respond. But hold on—some of the questions are new and have not been fully considered. You feel your body chemistry change. Blood pressure and heart rate go up as you seek to have all the answers and defend your position. The mood of the meeting also turns, it becomes argumentative as you become impatient with the questions. You can feel yourself being defensive. After all, you are the one who is the expert, they should be listening to you. The meeting does not go well.

What Happened Was a Brain Hijack

In simple terms you were the victim of a hijack. Your brain hijacked your mind.[78] The questions you couldn't answer were a stimulus interpreted by the brain as a threat—and it could "take no chances." It instantaneously activated the fear response as it sought to shoot first and ask questions later with the fight-or-flight response. A sudden flood of chemicals was released in your body to get you ready for the fight. Heart rate and blood pressure increased, pupils dilated to take in as much light as possible, muscles tensed up and non-essential systems were shut down, including blood flow to logic circuits. All were designed to help you survive a dangerous situation. If only you could have taken a step back to the slower pathway depicted in Figure 15-1.

Figure 15-1

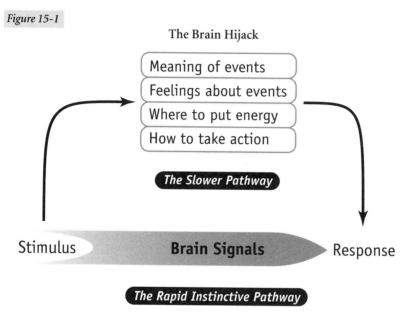

The Brain Hijack

- Meaning of events
- Feelings about events
- Where to put energy
- How to take action

The Slower Pathway

Stimulus **Brain Signals** Response

The Rapid Instinctive Pathway

Between Stimulus and Response is a Choice

Decisions occur in the space between stimulus and response. We don't commonly give much thought to what happens in our brain and mind in this space. However, when we reflect on our thoughts we have an improved chance of making better decisions and choices so that we can predict and avoid problems due to mind-bugs. The approach presented in the following chapters brings awareness of this space through a number of simple-to-use practices. It allows us to cultivate the ability to compensate for the weaknesses of our programmed ways of thinking and reacting.

Figure 15-2

The Space between Stimulus and Response

Stimulus ▶ Response

Keeping It Simple

As we consider solutions to avoiding mind-bugs, we are faced with a compelling challenge: the conditions of the typical corporate environment. If you live there you know how difficult things can be. Demand exceeds capacity. There is not enough time. There are not enough resources. People are typically stressed and stretched to the max. So, it is no surprise they avoid anything that takes more time or effort. On the other hand, if they learn to avoid mind-bugs, time spent on redoing and repairing damage will be reduced. That's why I offer a solution that can be incorporated easily. It is not a burdensome process to apply on top of everything else. It is the way we should go about the routines we do already.

**Reflecting does not just mean to stop and think.
It means to reflect on the quality of our thoughts, feelings,
and desires before we make decisions.**

Chapter 16:
The Solution—A Path to Better Decisions

Only One Person Stops You from Seeing the Path — You

＝ ＝ ＝ ＝ ＝ ＝ ＝ ＝ ＝ ＝ ＝ ＝ ＝ ＝ ＝ ＝

In Section One we learned that our conscious and non-conscious decisions determine how, when, and where we take action. With every action we take comes a risk. That is why the Chinese symbol for risk also means opportunity. We also learned there are two ways to do everything we do in life:

Figure 16-1

The Two Ways to Do Everything

The Two Ways:	My behavior is:	I am:	Mind-Bugs:
1. I am in command of my thoughts	Reflective	Mindful	Avoided
2. My thoughts are in command of me	Reactive	Mindless	Thrive

In Command of My Thoughts

When in command of our thoughts we are in a state of mindfulness. We are aware that our understanding of a situation is always subject to alternative explanations and are willing to direct our thought toward creating those other possibilities. Rather than over-committing to our original decisions and creating blind spots, we reflect on them. We are flexible and understand that there are many ways to view reality. We must be in command of our thinking in order to address the question: Where could a mind-bug manifest itself in my thinking and how can it be avoided?

My Thoughts are in Command of Me

When in a mindless state, we allow our mind to get "hooked" or attached to the many thoughts that arise randomly.[79] We are unknowingly under the command of those thoughts. We operate with habitual reactions and don't examine or observe the processes of our thoughts and their effects on decisions. It is easy for others to spot, as we are often diverted from rationality by our need to think well of ourselves, getting engulfed in a swamp of defensiveness and counterproductive thoughts. Even though the level of conflict may not be unacceptably high, unbiased decisions may be prevented because the perception of personal threat closes off options and survival mechanisms kick in.[80] As we lack the motivation or attention needed to avoid them, mind-bugs thrive in this environment. A by-product of this critical way of being is that we suffer from fatigue by rehearsing future and past events and clutter our minds, which increases stress.[81]

A Process to Take Command of Our Thinking

Before continuing it should be made clear that I am not suggesting mindfulness is something that should be aspired to in all situations. Many automatic behaviors, like learning to drive or other skills, are necessary, otherwise we would be overloaded with thinking about each step all the time—an overwhelmingly stressful and impossible situation. However, there are other times that we need to be in command of our thoughts so that mind-bugs do not subconsciously cause our decisions to crash. Knowing how to choose a mindful state by following a process reduces the threat of mind-bugs.

Inserting a Mental Breakpoint

One problem we face is that our thoughts about the basis for our decisions remain more constant than the actual basis itself. We can unknowingly get "dug in" and it is likely that paying attention may be trickier than we assume. You see, our thoughts influence how we physically see things and how we physically see things in turn influences our thoughts.[82] Even when we are mindful, it is only a temporary state.[83] It varies based on the situation, people, competitive thoughts, workload, and stress. Preventing this cycle requires an interruption I call a mental breakpoint.[84] Just like a software programmer, we can install a breakpoint to halt our decision process to examine it for bugs. And then we debug it. You will soon see that we can do this in a simple manner by asking carefully crafted questions.[85] We can turn looking for mind-bugs into a mindful process that can be deployed with all decisions both large and small.

Avoiding Mind-Bugs by Asking Questions

When people are required to make major decisions, defensive behavior as a result of mind-bugs is probably the most pervasive pattern as well as the most difficult to prevent or correct.[86] So, avoiding mind-bugs requires a systematic, impersonal, non-defensive way of asking ourselves and others questions with the purpose of revealing mind-bugs. By learning about mind-bugs in advance, we remove many subconscious personal threats. Through identifying the problem as something other than us, we can recognize and debug without personal attachment to our thoughts. Removing mind-bugs results in eliminating our attachments to our thoughts. Thinking is a skill. Asking these questions requires us to think about our thoughts. It is a higher level skill. Once revealed, mind-bugs can be avoided. In fact, they tend to scatter on their own.

The Six Steps on the Path to Better Decisions

Inserting a series of mental breakpoints creates space between stimulus and response so that we can choose our state of mind. Figure 16-2 provides the process by introducing the six steps on the Path to Better Decisions. Following it results in improved decisions, actions, and quality of life. The key for each step is to recognize if we are in command of our thinking. This chapter summarizes the steps. The next chapters will provide details and techniques to follow the path. Underlying this approach is our recognition that people are better off using simple methods well, rather than a complex method poorly.

Figure 16-2

The Six Step Path to Better Decisions

Step Six is to Begin Again at Step One

The Six Steps

Step One: Take command of my own thinking

Determining my own state of mind is the starting point and the foundation for avoiding mind-bugs and improving decisions. Nothing else can begin to be useful if I am mindless and reactive when making decisions. Since mindfulness is a temporary state, I must always begin by determining my state of mind.

Step Two: Practice mindful interactions with others

Our relationships require mindfulness if we are to work together effectively. Being in command of my thinking and helping others be in command of theirs helps us identify creative and innovative solutions and make good decisions about the way our teams interact.

Step Three: Take command of the way I learn and teach

We can make decisions free of mind-bugs only if we avoid mindless reactive and defensive behavior in the way we learn. Similarly, we can only help people grow if we do so in a way that does not invite reactivity. We must help, not hinder, the mindful way. Being in command of our learning and teaching is part of the way we avoid mind-bugs in decisions. It is also the way we grow as a person and a productive employee.

Step Four: Take command of business decisions

Our own actions and those of the groups we belong to lead to higher level business decisions. These involve change of all shapes and sizes—ranging from investment to downsizing. To reduce risk in these decisions we must avoid mind-bugs.

Step Five: Take command of the way I take and give correction

When things go wrong correction is required—and things will go wrong on occasion. We can look at this in two ways. When we chose mindfulness, we take and give correction in ways that generate action to correct the problems, not defensive behavior. When we react mindlessly, we often generate action that perpetuates the problem or even has the unintended consequence of creating a new one.

Step Six: Begin Again at Step One

Step Six is based on the realization and acceptance that The Path to Better Decisions is a journey, not a destination. It is a state of mind and not a permanent characteristic. We take what we have learned and apply it again to Step One, which is why I use a circle in the graphic, rather than tiered levels of achievement. This is not something to acquire like a merit badge; it is a way of life.

The Possibilities are Endless

One reason for Step Six is that mind-bugs change depending on the situation. As conditions vary, so do mind-bugs. Every interaction, every circumstance, and every judgment is unique and so are the mind-bugs that present themselves. Each relationship is based on what we are relating to at the time and who is doing the relating. Each is a unique state with its own features, individual influences, group factors, and decision options. Since conditions are nearly infinite, the possibilities for mind-bugs are endless. That's why tools like personality profiles taken once every 5-10 years are useless in identifying mind-bugs that could affect today's specific decisions. Other tools and practices are required to address our regularly changing states.

It is Easy to Fool Ourselves

Vulnerability to mind-bugs is situational. Those that occur under one specific set of conditions (i.e. state) may not be present under others. And those that present themselves under one aspect of a relationship may be absent under other conditions. Don't be fooled into thinking you have mastered your mind-bugs. One skillful moment of clarity does not eliminate vulnerability. To improve the quality of our thinking we must be on the lookout for mind-bugs in every decision and action.

It is what we learn after we think we know it all that really counts.

Step 1: Improving My Own Thinking

Aware of problems in my thinking, I have the power to fix them.

You have learned that when we are ignorant of the existence of our own mind-bugs, poor decisions and behaviors can thrive. The trouble is that we do not know our thoughts are a significant part of problems we face. Step One helps us grow in our own thinking. Sometimes that it is all that is required to fix a problem.

How to Begin

Whether you realize it or not, you have already taken the first step by reading this book. It serves as a mental breakpoint, however you have chosen to go about it. Just doing this will likely improve the quality of your thoughts. However, the book itself is a tool and can be used in many ways. Here are a few; you will likely think of many others.

1. Note and date the parts of this book that are most relevant to what is going on in your life right now: your problems, decisions, and personal interactions. What mind-bugs are surfacing in those par-

ticular situations? Where is your thinking in command of you? How can you improve your thinking?

2. Let someone else know about this book and that it is meaningful in helping your thinking. Suggest that they read the book and let you know what comes up for them in specific situations in their life. Work together on taking command of your thinking.

3. Think of someone else in your life with whom you may be having difficulties and note and date parts of the book you believe are important to your interaction. What is the context of your difficulty? What mind-bugs are surfacing? How can you improve your thinking?

4. Ask the other person in #3 to read the book and note and date parts of the book they believe are important to your relationship. How can you improve your thinking based on items they identified?

5. Meet and discuss the items recognized above with the person in #3. Try to figure out how you can both improve your thinking based on items identified.

Inserting a Mental Breakpoint

Awareness that we have a problem is critical to improvement. Our awareness is facilitated, in part, by pondering how we or our group might behave if we are infected with mind-bugs as it relates to specific situations. Pausing to reflect provides a moment of mindfulness, a space between stimulus and response, a mental breakpoint.

The following tool was developed to help each of us to become more aware of how our subconscious thoughts affect our actions. It is available in automated form free on our website (http://curecorporatestupidity.com).

The Mind-Bugs Awareness Index (MBA Index)

Figure 17-1 on the next page is a collection of statements about your experience regarding a particular situation. First write down the situation in the space provided below. Then, in relationship to the situation identified, consider how frequently or infrequently you currently have each experience shown in figure 17-1. Please answer according to what really reflects your experience rather than what you think your experience should be. Please treat each item separately from every other item.

Score each one in the corresponding box according to the following ratings guideline. Feel free to ponder each question but don't spend more than a few minutes on each. Total your score to get your MBA Index and then use the guidelines to assess your progress.

1. *First describe the specific situation you want to analyze. It could be a relationship with a person or group, some work you are doing, a decision, or other circumstance:*

_____

_____

_____

_____

2. *Next reflect on your experiences in Figure 17-1 and rate each one according to this scale:*

Ratings Guidelines

Frequency (% of the time)	Ratings
Always	5
Very Frequently	4
Sometime	3
Very Infrequently	2
Never	1

Figure 17-1

Mind-Bugs Awareness Index Evaluation Scorecard[87]

	Behavior	Rating: 1-5
1	I act in ways that discourage questioning of my views and robust challenge of the assertions that I make.	
2	I am inclined to avoid exploring and disclosing possible gaps and inconsistencies in my thinking, advice, and recommendations.	
3	I tend to blame others or the system and distance myself from responsibility for error.	
4	When I feel misunderstood, I first seek to explain my point of view before going any further.	
5	I am inclined to be less candid when the issues at stake are embarrassing, threatening, or risky for me personally.	
6	I consider massaging and/or censoring information if I believe it will help me.	
7	I don't check with others to see if my communication is inconsistent or ambiguous.	
8	I tend to avoid seeking and reflecting on feedback from others regarding the impact of my behavior.	
9	I do not change my mind without a struggle, even when given proper evidence.	
10	I tend to blow off ideas that are not consistent with my own point of view before evaluating them.	
11	I find it difficult to accept that primary responsibility for solving problems I face at work lies first with me.	
	Total (MBA) Index Score	

In Figure 17-2 are the guidelines for progress based on your score. The chapters in this section will help you grow in your awareness, improvement, and leadership.

Figure 17-2

Awareness Index Guide

Index Score	Level
35-55	Chronically Unaware
29-34	Mostly Unaware
23-28	Growing but major gaps exist
12-22	Strength much of the time but blind spots can exist
11	High Awareness Level

Contemplation is Exercise for the Mind

Spend time thinking about your lowest scores and work on your weakest areas. Ponder the Mind-Bug Reference Chart and identify those where you are currently most vulnerable in this situation. Take responsibility and hold yourself accountable to grow in your awareness. You will find that it will help you improve decisions, relationships, and your career. And, as a by-product, your life will be sweeter.

But Shouldn't I Just Trust My Gut?

One of the most important questions facing decision makers is when they should trust their gut instincts. My research and personal experience suggests that we cannot and should not try to prevent gut instincts from influencing our judgments. They access our accumulated experience for which meaning is created by our thoughts, feelings, desires, and past decisions. We start to feel something, often before we are conscious of having thought anything. And many times our instincts are correct—but not always.[88]

The Problem with Trusting our Gut

Problems can arise when our accumulated experience contains mind-bugs. Our brain draws conclusions and takes shortcuts in the way it interprets events and stores them for automated retrieval. These may be grounded in reality or misguided beliefs, rational interpretations or "emotional hijacking," relevant experience or faulty interpretation. I am not advocating "never trust your gut," only that it is sometimes a hiding place for mind-bugs. The only cure is to look for mind-bugs everywhere, including your gut instincts. Sound instincts will always stand up to scrutiny, while mind-bugs will tell us it is not worth looking for them!

Free yourself from ineffective habitual thoughts and behaviors that block improved decisions.

Moving from Step 1 to Step 2:
The Two Questions about the Two Ways

*There is nothing more powerful
than the ability to question our own thinking.*

If we are exploring our own mind-bugs and accepting that we all have them, then we are sufficiently ready to move on to Step Two. We don't have to be perfect, only aware.

Questions

As a reminder, avoiding mind-bugs requires a systematic, impersonal, non-defensive way of asking ourselves and others questions with the purpose of revealing mind-bugs. By inserting a mental breakpoint to ask these questions, we create space between stimulus and action. In this space, we take command of our thinking. Moving from Step One to Step Two requires getting comfortable with questions about our thinking.

The Two Questions about the Two Ways

You can ask two questions about anything in life and receive benefit because they provide a mental breakpoint to promote mindfulness, which is being in command of our thinking. There are many ways to ask the two questions based on the following table, but they all provide the same benefit. Here are a few examples. Choosing which works best depends on the situation. In some cases you will note that knowledge of mind-bugs is not even required.

Being in command of our thinking:

1. How would I do this if I am not in command of my thinking?	*2. How would I do this if I am in command of my thinking?*

Reflecting on how things could go wrong:

1. What does this meeting (decision, etc.) look like if things do not go well?	*2. What does it look like if things go well?*

Focus on mind-bugs

1. How could mind-bugs cause problems with this decision (meeting, etc.)?	*2. How will I avoid the mind-bugs that can cause problems?*

Reflecting on the elements of thought

1. How could faulty thoughts, feelings, and desires contribute to bad decisions?	*2. How will I identify and avoid faulty thoughts, feelings, and desires that contribute to bad decisions?*

The two questions work best when asked as early as possible in a project, meeting, relationship, decision, contemplated action, etc. But it is never too late to benefit. Merely questioning ourselves about The Two Ways helps to identify and avoid mind-bugs.

The Two Ways between People

As you can see in the following diagram, the complexity increases when there are two people involved. Not only does each person either react or reflect, but one person's response may become another's stimulus.

Figure 18-1

Stimulus and Response between People

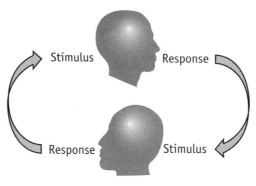

The Invitation

What do we invite in others if our response is reactive in our communications to someone else? Of course, a reactive response invites the same in others. Anger is most always met with more anger, attacking invites defensiveness, and justifying who is right invites more of the same. This is the dreaded "mind-bug spiral." It can be fatal. We have all experienced it sometime in our life. People just leave in anger, feign agreement but undermine cooperation, or much worse.[89]

Breaking the Mind-Bug Spiral

If two people are caught in a mind-bug spiral, where does it end? We all know people who don't speak to each other after decades of living this way, or departments in organizations that refuse to authentically help each other. We all have mind-bugs; no exceptions. They can create huge burdens. A mindful response is the only way out because it invites mindfulness in others. What kind of invitation do you prefer? What kind do you give? Here is a simple idea—learn to not accept an invitation to be reactive! We do this by being in command of our thinking versus allowing it to be in command of us. Insert a mental breakpoint and look for your own mind-bugs in how you are reacting. Create space to reflect before responding. If others continue to be reactive, at least we will not add to everyone's burden.

Listening is a Challenge

True listening requires taking command of our thinking. The simple fact is that we can't listen when we are reacting. There is no space for it. If the implications weren't so serious and the pain so great, it would be laughable to watch two people trying to reach an understanding by not listening to each other. Both are miserable and the mind-bugs and attorneys love it!

This is what most of us do when we are in a disagreement—we stop listening. It is like we carry around a pair of earplugs and the minute somebody starts saying something we don't like, we stuff them in our ears until they are done.[90] And while we are not listening, we are mentally getting ourselves ready to react with authority—to either attack, defend, or disengage. Of course we don't have time to listen, we are already thinking about something else.

Dealing with Disagreement

An effective way of dealing with a disagreement is simply to listen with complete attention. We can be mindful and seek to understand another's point of view even if we don't care for what the other person is saying. We are actually displaying a far greater power than arguing, the power to be in command of our thinking no matter how strongly we may initially disagree. No one can force us to react; that is our choice. We can take our non-conscious reaction and make it conscious by taking command of our thinking. If we take the choice away from our mind-bugs and hold it to the light for examination, we will make wiser decisions.

The Secret

The secret to resolving and avoiding conflicts in our life is to insert a mental breakpoint—to pause and consider the role of our own thoughts, feelings, and desires in the situation. The pause is a mental breakpoint. The secret to the secret is "we can't fake mindfulness." Try pretending to listen to someone—it doesn't work and they know it. The next time you find yourself arguing with someone, watch and listen with some detachment from your own thinking. You may be surprised at the result.

Using the Two Questions – An Example

Suppose that you had a difficult performance review to give to one of your direct reports. You know he has potential but needs to grow in certain areas or he may develop a fatal flaw. How could you use the "Two Questions" to avoid reaction and conflict and create a discussion where you are both in command of your thinking? Here is an example that follows the "Path to Better Decisions".

Step One
Take Command of Your Own Thinking

Ask yourself; how would you prepare for this performance review if you were in command of your thinking? Some ideas:

- Prepare by having no mind-bugs in the sufficiency and accuracy of your information, or in any beliefs or social pressures in giving specific feedback and help.
- Be concerned about performance and prepare to help as opposed to judge. Don't let your mind-bugs try to tell you that this is a "check the box" exercise.
- If he can't improve, it won't be because you are reactive and mindless. You are helpful and reflective.

Step Two
Practice Mindfulness in Your Interaction

Ask yourself: how you would both prepare for the performance review if you were both in command of your thinking? Some ideas:

- Send the invitation for him to respond with mindfulness. Well before the performance review, sit down with your employee and talk about the two questions as they relate to the review. This is the context against which mind-bugs should be considered.

- Make sure he has read this book and contemplated his own mind-bugs as it relates to this review. He should come prepared to present and discuss them.
- Ask how he would want you to deliver his review? Let him know your thoughts from Step One and how you will prepare for the review, not just "check the box."
- Ask him how he can practice being in command of his thinking in the way he prepares and receives the performance review.

Step Three:
Take Command of the Way You Learn and Teach

Ask yourself; how would you use this performance review to give feedback if you were both in command of your thinking? Some ideas:

- You will do your best to provide feedback in a way that does not invite reactivity. Your employee will work to avoid interpreting feedback in a defensive manner. You have both prepared in a way to avoid mind-bugs.
- He knows because you conducted Step Two that you put significant time into preparing for the review and have looked inside yourself first. He has done the same. So, he should come with a mindful attitude that you are trying to help him grow. You are not attacking him so there is nothing to defend.
- He should lay his mind-bugs on the table for you both to discuss. Consider and reflect together on how they might create a problem in accepting your feedback and in ways he needs to change. This will be easier because you have both done your homework in a mindful way.
- Avoid choosing to interpret any signals from him in a reactive manner, just take the time to reflect and consider.
- A performance review is one way you help people grow. It is also the way you learn to grow as a person and productive employee. Teaching and learning often go hand in hand.

The Symmetry

Recognize there are many levels of symmetry involved: how we prepare and how we conduct, how we interpret and how we react, how we speak and how we listen. We must always consider that we cannot react and be in command of our thinking at the same time. When in doubt, or you feel the chemicals flowing, insert a mental breakpoint, pause to reflect. Give better decisions a chance to shine through.

Other Examples of the Two Questions

- How would I collect and present data on a project for the CEO if I am in command of my thinking?
- How would the CEO request and receive data if she is in command of her thinking?
- How would two groups of people conduct a meeting if they are in command of their thinking?
- How would I approach someone I thought "threw me under the bus in a meeting" if I am in command of my thinking?
- How would I do any of the above if I am not in command of my thinking?

The Way We Conduct Our Work

This one simple practice should become part of all activities. It is not something on top of our work, it is the way we conduct our work when we are in command of our thinking. When answered objectively The Two Questions will help identify and avoid mind-bugs. They will save time, avoid problems, and reduce risk in everything we do. We will see more specific examples in the upcoming chapters.

The Two Ways in Groups

When groups of people interact, the chance for mind-bugs grows exponentially. That's because one person's response can be a stimulus to many others. Figure 18-2 demonstrates the problem far better than words. It shows why this principle is the basis for social networks such as Facebook and Twitter.

It is also important to note that we can be in command of our thinking in some relationships and situations while reactive and out of control in others. Mind-bugs are situational. Don't trust that because you are mindful at one moment that mind-bugs have been eradicated. They continue to present themselves whenever we are mindless.

Figure 18-2

Stimulus and Response in Groups

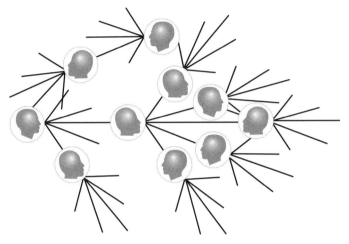

The Two Ways and Defensive Reasoning

As we have previously mentioned, one problem with mind-bugs is that they cause defensive reasoning, effectively preventing their discovery. When we are not in command of our thinking, we are likely to either resist asking The Two Questions based on our defensive and self-justifying reasons, or our answers are just "lip service" to prove we are following the path. Either way, if someone else observes this behavior and offers advice, look out—here come your defensive mind-bugs.

So be prepared to have your mind-bugs surface and tell you The Two Questions are a waste of time or that your other processes have this covered. You are only trying to fool yourself. If you are having these sensations right now, the urge to deny the value of these two simple questions, that's evidence of a mind-bug at work. Meet your mind-bugs head on and objectively ask The Two Questions:

1. How will I practice becoming aware of my mind-bugs when I am in command of my thinking?

2. How will I practice becoming aware of my mind-bugs when my thinking is in command of me?

When you feel compelled to use an excuse or rationalize away not asking the questions, stop and think about why you feel that way. This will provide a mental breakpoint and you will become aware that you no longer need to react that way. Then pause and become aware of your new mindfulness. You are starting to take command.

The Two Ways and Bad Bosses

One thing most bad bosses have in common is lack of awareness that they're bad bosses. Under the influence of mind-bugs, nobody wants to believe they are the problem. Yet the only way out is to own the problem; only then do we have the power to fix it. When it's happening to us, we engage our defensive reasoning. And not only is that bad for decisions, it's bad for careers as well. So, even if we are convinced of being the greatest manager around, we would still be wise to check for mind-bugs. Of course that cuts two ways. Taking a long hard look in the mirror before pointing fingers at others is a sign of being in command of our thinking. That is the symmetry.

One Size Does Not Fit All

Remember what I said earlier, vulnerability to mind-bugs is situational. Those that occur under one specific set of conditions may not be present under others. And those that present themselves under one aspect of a relationship may be absent in others. Don't be fooled into thinking you have mastered your mind-bugs. One skillful moment of clarity does not eliminate vulnerability. To improve the quality of our thinking we must be on the lookout for mind-bugs in every decision and action.

The Danger:
One spasm of mindfulness does not make us mindful.
Mind-bugs will want us to believe it does.

Step 2: Improving Interaction in Groups

*A group becomes a true team when each member
is in command of his thinking.*

⏐ ⏐ ⏐ ⏐ ■ ■ ■ ■ ■ ■ ■ ■ ■ ■ ■ ■ ⏐ ⏐ ⏐ ⏐

Step Two is about your interaction with others. All individuals and groups are vulnerable to mind-bugs in behaviors and decisions. Much of the time we are blind to their existence and also blind to the fact we are blind.[91] These practices help us gain awareness of our blind spots and reduce breeding grounds for mind-bugs.

Tool: Group De-bugging

Meet with a group of people with whom you are working to deliver results. Identify a specific result you are working to deliver together. Distribute individual copies of the Mind-Bug Reference Chart found in Chapter 14 and reproduced again here for your convenience. As it relates to the specific result:

1. Have each person identify the top three mind-bugs where each believes they are personally most vulnerable as it relates to this result.

2. Have each person identify the top three mind-bugs where each believes the group is most vulnerable.

3. Discuss the mind-bugs as a group.

4. Identify how the mind-bugs could cause problems.

5. Identify how to avoid problems and help decisions go right.

6. Have fun with the discussions.

Mind-Bug Reference Chart

Dimensions, Mind-Bugs, and Definitions		
Sufficiency	Informed Leader Fallacy	A belief by a leader that he/she is better informed and has better instincts than others, simply because he/she is the leader.
	Source Influence	Determining level of sufficiency depending on the source.
	Assumption Error	Basing decisions on assumptions we believe are true, without challenging those assumptions.
	Snap Judgment Defense	Defending decisions made on solely on snap judgment.
	Shooting the Critics	The tendency to marginalize people who disagree with us.
Accuracy	Unverified Information vs Fact	Causes us to confuse unverified information with facts.
	Generalization without Evidence	Making generalizations without the evidence to back them up.
	Seeing Patterns that are not Real	Seeing patterns in random data when none exist.
	Data Rejection	A reflex-like rejection of new facts because they contradict existing norms.
	Data Favoritism	Selecting, using and favoring data in a self-serving, unquestioning way.

Beliefs	Outcome Attachment	Being so attached to outcomes that serve our interest that we fail to look for problems in our thinking and decisions.
	Shortcomings Denial	Underestimating our own shortcomings by not believing we have them and rationalizing and assuming we can control them.
	Closed Mind	The inability to hold and examine two opposing views at the same time and to be closed to other perspectives than ours.
	Experience Bias	Believing that future events will occur in a specific way based on our prior experience, and not seeing conditions differ.
	Competency Blindness	Believing others are competent in areas when they are not and vice versa when it suits our subconscious needs.
Social	Conforming Error	Subconsciously conforming our thinking to the thinking of our group.
	Rose Colored Glasses	Overestimating the likelihood of positive events because everyone in the group believes they will happen.
	Power Insulation	The power structure discourages disturbances to group beliefs.
	Status Quo	Sticking to the status quo and creating significant friction that works against new ideas.
	Hiding Weaknesses	The tendency to hide our weaknesses by presenting the most favorable picture to outsiders.

Example

For many years Apex Products (a hypothetical company) had been selling their goods through large distributors with solid financial characteristics. After their annual strategic planning process, the Apex leadership team believed the market was changing and they needed to sell direct to the end customer and eliminate the middle man. While profit margins would be higher and they would benefit from direct relationships with the user, individual account size would decrease and numbers increase, and there would be a greater burden on the credit department. Sales was afraid that Credit would become the sales prevention department. Credit was afraid of how they would look with greater write-offs. Leadership was concerned that each would lobby for power over the other and increase risk. They felt learning about mind-bugs might result in better decisions and outcomes.

The team members for both departments were quickly taught about the Mind-Bug Reference Chart by the consultant brought in to help with change management. They met together and reviewed the goal established by Apex Products leadership. Then each person identified the top three mind-bugs that each believed they were most vulnerable to as it related to achieving the company goal. They ranked them and pinpointed the top three mind-bugs for each group.

Credit prioritized their mind-bugs as: Generalization without Evidence, Assumption Error, and Status Quo. Pointing to mind-bugs, rather than themselves, made it easier to see how they could non-consciously resist the change based on false assumptions and justify their view based on generalizations. Sales identified with: Source Influence, Rose Colored Glasses, and Shooting the Critics. They could see how much they wanted to please leadership and how easy it was to fall into the trap of presenting overly optimistic numbers while shooting the credit department if they dared criticize.

The teams held a robust discussion with leadership and openly presented where the mind-bugs were hiding and what things might look like if the mind-bugs reigned. Rather than defending their turf, the teams went about identifying how to avoid problems from mind-bugs and help decisions go right. Cooperation flourished and the team members began calling out mind-bugs in real time when they surfaced in discussions.

Avoiding Blind Spots

Blind spots occur when we believe that we are more in command of our thinking than is actually the case. When this occurs we are blind to problems our decisions can create and blind to the fact that we are blind. Others can help us take command of our thinking by helping us identify our blind spots. Here is just one approach to avoiding this problem.

Identify and meet with a group of people with whom you are working to achieve specific results. Ask them to evaluate you with the MBA Index scorecard from Chapter 17 against those results and then average their scores. Compare their score to yours and determine the difference.

The more their score for you is higher than yours, the bigger your blind spot and greater your chance of poor decisions.

To reduce your blind spot and increase your chance of good decisions, take the following actions:

1. Talk to the group or individuals about your blind spots without being defensive and learn how you can improve and eliminate the blindness.
2. What mind-bugs could be present? Bring them up and discuss them in meetings. Refer to them in groups whenever you are making decisions.

Only when we are connected to ourselves can we effectively connect to others.

Step 2 Continued: The Two Ways of Interacting with Others

The greatest problem with communication
is thinking it has been done.

— *Bernard Shaw*

Many decisions are grounded in communications and relationships with others. How we speak, listen, write, and emote are all decisions that we make. These are the not-so-small decisions that feed the big decisions. But, these decisions generally go unnoticed until problems develop. Then we spend time correcting problems that could have been avoided in the first place.

Relationships and the Invitation to be Reactive

Think of the relationships you have at work with your manager, team mates, employees, and outside parties. Are these relationships mindful or mindless? One of the things we can't see when we are mindless is that we are mindless. Whichever "way" we are is an invitation to others to be the same way. If we are reactive, we invite reactivity in others. Others respond to our "state of mind."

Mindless Groups

Mindless groups can create defensiveness, self-fulfilling prophecies, closed processes, and escalating error. All of these, in turn, reinforce the need for:

- being in unilateral control
- winning and not losing
- suppressing negative feelings
- appearing rational
- projecting blame for errors on others and on the system

You may say, "Organizations always have these problems." "Mind-bugs", I say!

Avoiding Mind-Bugs in Meetings

In order to avoid mind-bugs in meetings it is helpful to have a pre-meeting discussion based on The Two Questions.

1. How would we conduct this meeting if we are not in command of our thinking?	*2.* How would we conduct this meeting if we are in command of our thinking?

For example, if we are not in command of our thinking, the following might take place:

- Individuals might push for their own outcome, over that which is best for the company.
- Team members might withhold information if it could possibly sway decisions away from their own self-interest.
- A request for more information might be interpreted as an attack.
- Questions may go unasked for fear of being put down.

To the contrary, if we are in command of our thinking, the following might take place:

- Individuals would put aside self-interest for what is best for the company.

- We would be open to the new ideas of those in a different department. We even seek them out.
- We mindfully challenge the opinions of those in power, without fear of negative repercussions.
- Cooperation flourishes

You will want to refer to the four dimensions and mind-bug descriptions to get the conversation going. The odds of avoiding mind-bugs in a group setting increase when discussion of them brings them to our attention.

Avoiding Mind-bugs in Communications

Communicating with others whether it by phone, email, text, snail mail, or otherwise creates breeding grounds for mind-bugs. The faster the response, the more mindless we become. Everyone has experienced being misunderstood when we thought our intentions were clear. And yikes— the messes we can inadvertently create when this happens. If we only insert a mental breakpoint by pausing to ask ourselves two simple questions, we give better decisions a chance to flourish:

1. How would I (we) communicate this message if I (we) are not in command of my (our) thinking?

2. How would I (we) communicate this if I (we) are in command of my (our) thinking?

Be sure to do this before you hit the send key on all your texts and emails!

Group Culture Awareness

Each person in a group should take the MBA Index scorecard for themselves and also score the group as a whole. Compare individual scores to the group and look for blind spots between how people rate themselves versus the group. When individual ratings are better than how they perceive their own group, mind-bugs like Shortcomings Denial and Competency Blindness can wreak havoc with decisions. That's because these blind spots contain mind-bugs that can corrupt even the most noble decisions.

**The single most important question for a team is—
are we in command of our thinking as a group
or is our thinking in command of us?**

Step 3: Improving Learning and Feedback

In times of change learners inherit the earth,
while the learned find themselves beautifully equipped
to deal with a world that no longer exists.

— Eric Hoffer

Nothing lives without growth and change. It is a fact of nature that holds true with people, relationships, and organizations. It really is simple; the ability to learn is a huge advantage that has lead to the survival of our species. Yet we all know of businesses that failed because they did not learn to adapt to change. Most all of us know that problems occur when we fail to grow and change and yet that is the nature of mind-bugs——resistance. And they devise ingenious reasoning to justify our reaction, causing us to resist the very things that will help us survive in a changing world.

Learning

As humans, we vary in what we can individually learn depending on our own physical, mental, social, and personal characteristics. But I propose it is also true that learning is more effective when we are reflective and mindful. We best learn how to grow as a person and productive employee if we are in command of our thinking in the way we learn and avoid mindless reactive behavior.

Organizational Learning

Companies learn and grow because their employees do that as individuals and groups. Only then can they recognize the changes around them that lead to out of date or faulty assumptions and flawed decisions. We begin learning by seeking understanding of ourselves—by questioning ourselves in a mindful way.

Learning Awareness Index (LA Index)

Figure 21-1 provides a tool to learn about our learning. I call it the Learning Awareness Index (LA Index). It is a collection of statements about your experience regarding a particular learning situation. First write down the situation in the space provided. Then in relationship to the situation identified, consider how frequently or infrequently you currently have each experience shown in figure 21-1. Please answer according to what really reflects your experience rather than what you think your experience should be. Please treat each item separately from every other item.

Score each one in the corresponding box according to the following ratings guideline. Feel free to ponder each question but don't spend more than a few minutes on each. Total your score to get your LA Index and then use the guidelines to assess your progress. Have a group do the same to assess the organizational learning culture. Just make the appropriate changes in the questions to reflect the company as opposed to an individual.

1. *First describe the specific situation you want to analyze as it relates to your ability to learn and grow. It could be a relationship with a person or group, some work you are doing, a decision, or other circumstance:*

_____

_____

_____

_____

2. *Next reflect on your experiences in Figure 21-1 and rate each one according to this scale.*

Ratings Guidelines

Frequency (% of the time)	Ratings
Always	5
Very Frequently	4
Sometime	3
Very Infrequently	2
Never	1

Figure 21-1

Learning Awareness Index (LA Index)

	Behavior	Rating: 1-5
1	I tend to get lost in reactive, mindless, and internally congested behavior about my learning and growth.	
2	I often try to explain my feelings and point of view before I seek to understand ideas about training.	
3	I act in ways that discourage inquiry into my views and assertions that I make about my learning.	
4	I am inclined to avoid exploring and disclosing possible gaps and inconsistencies in my thinking, advice, and recommendations.	
5	I tend to avoid seeking and reflecting on feedback from others regarding the impact of my behavior.	
6	I do not change my mind without a struggle, even when given proper evidence.	
7	I tend to blow off ideas about my learning that are not consistent with my own point of view.	
8	I find it difficult to accept that primary responsibility for my learning, change, and growth lies first with me.	
	Total Learning Awareness Index (LAI) Score	

Learning Awareness Guide

Index	Learning Awareness
32-40	Resistant
25-32	Random
17-24	Growing but major gaps exist
9-16	Strength much of the time but blind spots can exist
8	Completely aware

The Two Questions about Learning

1. In what ways am I mindful and in control of my thinking in the way I learn and grow?

2. In what ways am I mindless and reactive in the way I learn and grow?

The Learning Awareness Index and The Two Questions will provide personal insight into the presence of mind-bugs that could negatively impact our ability to learn and grow.

Feedback

Feedback has two perspectives: someone giving and someone receiving. It is most effective when it is mindful in both directions. When giving feedback I prepare myself by asking The Two Questions:

1. How do I give feedback when I am in command of my thinking?

2. How do I give feedback when I am not in command of my thinking?

When I am receiving feedback I ask The Two Questions from another perspective:

1. How do I receive feedback when I am in command of my thinking?

2. How do I receive feedback when I am not in command of my thinking?

When the giver and receiver reflect on these questions together beforehand, feedback is set up to be a positive experience for both parties. (See the example in Chapter 20)

The Gift

One way to look at feedback is as a gift. I am either receiving the gift or giving it. It is the gift of growth, development, and awareness for the individual and improved performance for the company. In giving this gift, why would we ever be reactive? In receiving this gift why would we ever have a defensive mind set? Well—if mind-bugs are present.

Avoiding mind-bugs is a gift that benefits everyone.

Step 4: Decisions, The 30 Second Scan

Wisdom is not found in our thoughts—
It is in the space we create to think about our thoughts.

⊢ ⊦ ⊦ ⊦ ▪ ▪ ▪ ■ ■ ■ ■ ■ ▪ ▪ ⊦ ⊦ ⊦ ⊦

We can only make the best decisions if we are aware of our individual and group mind-bugs—period! Read that again and again until it is second nature. We are most effective in our move to Step Four when we are actively working on Steps One, Two, and Three. This is creating a mindful attitude where we take command of our thinking

Thinking and Decisions in Business

Significant thinking activities in business generate considerable stimuli and response. Planning, analysis, meetings, presentations, discussions, and decisions are all fueled largely by identification and preoccupation with thoughts, feelings, and desires. Faulty decisions can occur when our preoccupation with our thoughts is stronger than our ability to let go of them easily. The "30 Second Scan" was created in order to insert a mental breakpoint so that we become present with every decision. Pausing to question ourselves before deciding provides immediate access to the path to better decisions. Then we have a choice to be wise or something less.

Tool: The 30 Second Scan

For each decision we are about to make simply answer yes or no to the following.

Have we sufficiently considered …

1. … how the personal stake or vested interest for each person or group involved could influence this evaluation?

2. … how beliefs and desires may have colored or influenced any judgments or inferences?

3. … if there are any critical gaps in the sufficiency of the information used to support our arguments?

4. … what makes us confident that the data we are depending on is accurate?

5. … what mind-bugs may be present that could affect our judgment?

6. … if I should continue with this decision if my answer is no to any of the first five questions?

You will soon see that if the answer to question 6 is "no," then you are exposed to mind-bugs. Your mental processes require debugging. We show you how to do that in the next chapter.

Despite the facts that all decisions involve alternatives, values, and uncertainty and that all decision processes involve problem structuring and evaluation, decisions differ in important ways. Most obviously, decisions differ enormously in difficulty. Most, in fact, are trivial[92] and will not require further attention. But it's the ones that do that you can't afford to miss.

The "30 Second Scan" will substantially reduce risk for any decision we are about to make and will cultivate higher quality thinking. But it does require regular practice and commitment as mind-bugs will present themselves advising you that this is a waste of time. If that is coming up for you, meet your mind-bugs head on with this exercise and prove them wrong.

ı ı ı ı ı ı ■ ■ ■ ■ ▬ ▒ ▓ ■ ■ ■ ı ı ı ı ı

**We cannot appease our hunger by reading the menu.[93]
Just as we must eat, we must put words into practice.**

Step 4 Continued:
The Mind-Bug Debugging Process

Any sufficiently advanced software bug is indistinguishable from a feature.

— Rich Kulawiec

' ' ' ' ' ▪ ▪ ▪ ▬ ▬ ▬ ▬ ▪ ▪ ' ' ' ' '

Executives, managers, and supervisors often spend far more time fixing decisions that go wrong versus helping them go right. In many cases that's because there were mind-bugs in their decisions. I aim to help change that. Just like software is debugged, so can our decisions be debugged. When decisions go poorly, there will typically be a review of what went wrong and identification of lessons learned. But using an after-the-fact analysis is too late to be of any value. It is like shutting the screen door once the bugs are already in the house. And, mind-bugs work to prevent us from seeing the truth even in a post-mortem exercise. The "Mind-Bug Debugging Process" looks for mind-bugs *up front*, well before a final decision is made, funds are committed, and a project starts.[94] And, it serves as a platform from which to prevent them from wreaking havoc.

The Problem: Judgments Have Already Occurred

The challenge we all face is that even well before decisions are consciously made, other judgments have already non-consciously occurred. They are automatic[95] and mindless by their very nature. That's because the human mind is continually reacting to the environment by organizing, interpreting, forming impressions, establishing meaning, drawing conclusions, and developing a point of view as it seeks to perceive and understand its surroundings. We can't help it; it is just the way we are wired. We begin to do this from the moment we wake up every day. And we don't do this randomly. Our non-conscious judgments are aligned with our goals, desires, fears, needs, beliefs, values, self image, and interpretation of the social world around us. Errors occur when we non-consciously allow past interpretations to influence what is happening right now. Then we may become judgmental without being aware of it.[96] Only when we take command of our thinking can we change the way events or impressions were initially stored.

Approach

A typical pre-launch risk analysis is focused on everything that might go wrong with a decision in the future. Then it identifies potential options to address each one should it develop. The Mind-Bugs Debugging Process is very different. It inspects the current decision before it is finalized and predicts possible mind-bugs that may have shaped a lesser-quality decision. It is like debugging computer software before it is released, only it applies to our mental software. This gives us a chance to debug faults in the decision beforehand. It is one way we can spend more time up front helping decisions go well, and spend less time fixing those that go wrong.

Context Illuminates the Darkness

This principle refers to the most important information needed during debugging a decision: context. We sometimes forget that decisions are always made relative to a backdrop, that is, relative to the context from which they are made. Each is different, each is unique. To prepare for debugging we follow the same initial rule as software programmers. We identify how the decision is currently constructed. It is our mental program of reasoning and conclusions that lead to the decision of where to put our energy. In a sense, it is like the software code of a computer program.

To debug a decision for mind-bugs we must first stop and freeze its construct. Once we clarify the basis or construct for the decision, we can proceed to debug it.

The Decision Debugging Tool

In computer software the debugging tool is a separate program used to test the program of interest and eliminate bugs. The importance of a good debugging program cannot be overstated and is often the deciding factor for selecting a given language and platform. The absence of a debugging tool has been said to "make you feel like a blind man in a dark room looking for a black cat that isn't there".[97]

Debuggers are an indispensable tool in the development process. In fact, during the course of the average software project, more hours are spent debugging software than in compiling code. And yet, we spend precious little time debugging our human decisions. In our case, the main purpose of the debugger is to find faults in decisions due to mind-bugs. Because humans have already attempted to remove faults, the debugger finds those that have been missed. Just like corruptions exist in software execution, they also exist as thought corruption.

Tool: The Debugging Process

Here are the steps in the basic Mind-Bug Debugging process.

1. Insert mental breakpoints in the decision process.

   a. The team intentionally pauses to examine the current state of the decision.
   b. Everyone adopts an attitude that they are willing to investigate viewpoints that differ from their own with the goal of getting at the truth.

2. Clarify and agree on the decision construct[§§] to be used for debugging as follows:

---

§§ Note: This construct should be easy to come by, otherwise there is a critical gap in the decision process. In that case, taking the time to fully develop the decision construct will pay dividends on the quality of decisions. That said, it is beyond the scope of this

    a. What is the basic purpose of the decision?

    b. What are the conclusions that support this decision?

    c. What assumptions are you using to support each conclusion?

    d. What information are you using to support either the assumptions or conclusions directly?

3. Inspect and evaluate each conclusion one at a time along with the related assumptions, information, and any other reasoning."

    a. Using the mind-bug list, each team member identifies the mind-bugs they sense each conclusion is most susceptible to.

    b. The results are compiled by identifying the top 3-5 mind-bugs associated with each conclusion and sharing with the team.

4. Debug

    a. The team discusses the merits of each and how they can be avoided.

    b. The team discusses what important evidence may have been omitted or suppressed due to mind-bugs.

    c. The team determines if it should revise any of the arguments and how it will avoid mind-bugs.

5. Depending on the complexity and timeline, future breakpoints are established at preset conditions to insure new infection does not occur as the decision state changes.

From Hindsight to Foresight

The beauty of this practice is that rather than arguing and defending opinions and plans, team members now "look good" by thinking of how mind-bugs could be present. The dynamics change from trying to "spin information" in order to avoid anything that might be in conflict with a recommendation to working together to surface and avoid potential problems. When the Debugging Process becomes part of a culture, a company

---

book to teach critical thinking. Mind-bugs are critical thinking hindrances but only one aspect of critical thinking. See the appendix for several references in this area.

" Software programmers call this a stack back-trace.

moves from reacting with hindsight analysis to foresight—prevention through mindful investigation of mind-bugs.

An Example of the Debugging Process: Acquisition and Integration

Imagine Company A is planning to acquire Company B and justification is based in part on a decision to immediately shut down plants, eliminate many jobs, and gain perceived productivity. The Board wants to be sure that mind-bugs are not involved with the recommendation. Before any final decision to make the acquisition, the key players at Company A are trained on mind-bugs, then meet to conduct a decision Debugging Process. Here are some hypothetical steps and results:

1. Following the Debugging Process, Company A clarifies its stated purpose for the acquisition and integration and fully clarifies the decision construct. Being a large company with formal processes it is easy to extract the decision construct from the numerous analyses that already exist. Knowing that the Board will require the results ofthis exercise helps them make a serious effort and not just give it lip service.

2. Team members take the responsibility to look for mind-bugs in each of the arguments. They submit their individual sense of mind-bugs on a confidential basis. No one knows who submitted what.

3. Data is compiled and findings presented based on a ranking of the most relevant and impactful data. Some key results are:

    a. Based on the overall high ranking of Conforming Error, Power Insulation, and Outcome Attachment, it became clear that some knowledgeable individuals may have been "playing it safe".

    b. Shortcomings Denial, Experience Bias, and Data Favoritism also surfaced as concerns as related to market and product research used to justify the acquisition.

4. A robust group discussion is started by the leader.
   a. Now seeing the entire list, he asks each person to review a conclusion and mind-bug and why it should concern the team.
   b. The dialogue reveals an exposure to Outcome Attachment since they all had the sense Company A executives believed they needed this acquisition to be successful. The possibility also is uncovered that personal gain could influence attachment.
   c. This prompts an in-depth review of assumptions to make certain they are warranted and to determine if there are any strategic omissions.
   d. Since politics are not at play and discussions are reflective, team members are enthusiastically engaged in working together to surface and avoid potential problems. Indeed, Generalization without Evidence, along with Status Quo mind-bugs are highlighted and the benefits of the acquisition are seriously called into question.
   e. Cooperation flourishes.

Assuming the Debugging Process is Not Followed

How might mind-bugs have impacted the decision? Executives are attached to their pre-defined outcomes. Any challenge to thinking is met with defensiveness. Those that challenge are eventually marginalized. Data is used in a self-serving manner to support what team members interpret are leader's interests. The likelihood of positive events is overestimated because everyone wants them to happen. Other possibly valuable options are overlooked and desired options are erroneously validated. Individual and group defensiveness is the norm. Personal agendas and blame flourish when the acquisition does not meet expectations.

**Move from fixing decisions that go wrong
to helping them go right.**

Chapter 24

Step 5: Correction

When decisions go wrong ....

I I I I I I ■ ■ ■ ■ ■ ■ ■ ■ ■ I I I I I I

Things don't always go right. Performance problems develop, cooperation breaks down, mistakes get made, stress increases, motivation drops off, strategies don't pan out, execution is problematic, and targets get missed. All these and more call for correction. I propose a simple process based on the Six Steps to Better Decisions.

The Six Steps to Correction

Step One:

Have I been mindful in the way I take command of my thinking?

The first step is to consider my own thinking. Do I act in ways that are mindfully reflective or mindlessly reactive? How do I know? Have I used the tools and practices that will help me avoid mind-bugs? When my own actions are part of the problem, I need to take responsibility to correct myself before I will be effective correcting anything else. Many times recognizing and avoiding our own mind-bugs is all the correction that is needed.

Step Two:

Have I been mindful in the way I help and interact with others?

If I have faithfully stayed in command of my own thinking then I should examine my relationships with my boss, co-workers, employees, and outside parties. Do I regularly help these interactions be mindful?

Step Three:

Have we been mindful in the way we teach, learn, and give and receive feedback?

If we have not yet found the problem then it is time to examine the way we and others teach, learn, and give and receive feedback. Are we mindfully reflective or mindlessly reactive? Is there a fundamental problem in this area?

Step Four:

Have we been mindful in the way we make business decisions?

Have we practiced mind-bug detection in our decisions? Are we using the 30 Second Scan and the Debugging Process? Do we examine our thinking for mind-bugs as part of our decision process?

Step Five:

Correction

Having been through the steps and finding the problem still remains, we are ready to correct. Remember, a spasm of mindfulness does not make us mindful. And, excellence in one step does not compensate for failure elsewhere. Here is where The Two Questions will help us be prepared to correct others:

1. How do I correct others when I am in command of my thinking? | *2.* How do I correct others when I am not in command of my thinking?

Holding others accountable for performance is to be mindful of our expectations of them. Indulging others is a mindless action.

Step Six:
Review Step One

Correction of others is never effective unless we have been mindful of our own role in helping them succeed. Our expectations must be appropriate in light of our role in the problem.

Mindful Correction

When we are mindless and reactive, our correction may be general, unclear, blaming, punishing, angry, defensive, sarcastic, insulting, or even abusive. These corrections are of little help and only invite reactive behavior we either indulge or terminate.

When we are mindful and reflective, correction takes the form of very direct, specific, straightforward, well thought-out help or options. We are firm but with a spirit of encouragement. Because we have followed the six steps, we are mindful in the way we correct.

**We are not claiming to be perfect ourselves,
just mindful in our correction.**

Step 6: Using the Path to Better Decisions

Spending 80% of our time helping decisions go right.

In the last chapter we saw how to use The Six Step Path to Better Decisions in correction when problems occur. This chapter shows how to use this same tool in preventing problems.

Figure 25-1 points out that the first four steps are involved in helping decisions go right, while the fifth step is focused on dealing with problems.

Figure 25-1

The Six Step Path to Better Decisions Ratio

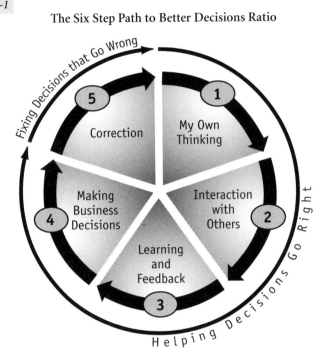

This implies that 80% of leadership, management, supervisor, team leader, and employee time should be spent helping make good decisions and only 20% of their time in fixing bad decisions. All too often this ratio gets reversed in corporations. To discover the reason we must look below the surface of our problems, at mind-bugs. Figure 25-2 lays out the tools and practices for each step.

Figure 25-2

Steps, Tools, and Practices*

Step	Description	Tools and Practices
1	Practice mindfulness in my own thinking	§ Read this book § MBA Index and Advanced MBA Index § The Two Questions § Mind-Bugs Reference Chart
2	Practice mindful interaction with others	§ Everyone reads and discusses this book § MBA Index and Advanced MBA Index § The Two Questions § Mind-Bugs Reference Chart
3	Practice mindfulness in learning and feedback	§ The Learning Awareness Index (LA Index) § The Two Questions
4	Make mindful decisions	§ 30 second scan § Decision Debugging Process
5	Be mindful in the way I take and give correction	§ The Six Steps § The Two Questions
6	Mindfully begin again at step one	§ Review the book § Use The Two Questions § Check progress and make corrections

Note: all tools and practices will have a home on our website at for additional features, applications, support, and feedback. Just go there at http://curecorporatestupidity.com

---

The path to better decisions begins with the first step.

Chapter 26: What Prevents the First Step?

Every journey we take begins where we are.

ı ı ı ı ı ■ ■ ■ ■ ■ ■ ■ ■ ■ ■ ■ ı ı ı ı ı

I can't overstate the importance of getting off to the right start. Like solving a problem, if assumptions are faulty then solutions will be unsound. Foundations of a building must be strong, otherwise the whole structure will topple in time. Fall crops depend on the initial steps taken in the spring. This book is intended to strike a keynote, which I hope will carry through to fulfillment and success. But just like a child learning to walk, success begins with the first step.

Even after a group has been prepared to work in this new way, they still need to start at the beginning. They need to develop skills and discipline through commitment and practice. We should anticipate the following general reactions.

Some are Ready

Some people are ready. They will identify with and accept "taking command of their thinking" openly and eagerly. They are the early adopters and are open-minded students. They meet the invitation to personal growth with reflection and eagerness.

Some are Unsure

Some people will react to this approach initially by resisting it; they react to the invitation as opposed to reflecting on it. They wait cautiously to see how things go before deciding what "side to take". Initially it may only be a resistance to change that is driven by their mind-bugs.

Some Resist

Some will resist because they have already assumed a reactive way of life as their path to success, be it the corporate ladder or personal interactions. They fear letting go of a strategy that has proven so successful—at least in their mind. And they are reluctant to admit they may have been wrong in the past. Mind-bugs are powerfully entrenched in this group.

Expect All of This

Most of us experience all three at one time or another and to one degree or another. Mind-bugs can be strong. Expect all of this and accept it mindfully. Most of us need some time, but if we are consistent in our efforts we will relax and trust the new direction. Once we can sustain this way of working for a while, most will intensify their efforts and commitment. That's because it pays off in so many ways.

The Key is Consistency

The key is consistency in "taking command of your thinking" through practice and leadership. I believe you can do nothing more important in your work and your life. By adopting these principles you can make a significant and lasting contribution to the results of your organization and to people's lives.

Company success depends on something more than the intelligence of its people.

Chapter 27:
The Age of Quality Thinking

Do we have the wisdom to build on the lessons of the past?
Or will mind-bugs continue to prevail?

I use the term mind-bugs as a metaphor for the problems all humans experience with thinking. That's because the concept becomes overly complex if described solely with the language available. To become aware of our mind-bugs means we no longer apply yesterday's business solutions to the problems of today. We no longer ignore the problems in our thinking, rather, we are conscious of them.

Corporate Consciousness

This book is about all of us. But I chose to focus on corporations because they have so much potential power. If that power can be channeled through a greater command of thinking, imagine the benefit that will result to the entire world. And, individuals can control corporations by their daily vote of whether or not to buy products and services. For example, engagement with sustainability is more than lip service for some large companies, because it is what the public wants, *and* it is a good idea for the future needs of the company itself.

So we see that corporate dysfunction *and* consciousness are *both* accelerating. Things are getting worse and better at the same time. But the dysfunction is more apparent because it makes better news.

Recognize the Problem

The most sweeping corporate governance reform in any country in five decades, the United States Sarbanes-Oxley Act (SOX) of 2002, was overwhelmingly passed by an emotional Congress in the wake of major corporate and accounting scandals and the popping of the Internet/telecom equity bubble. The bill was enacted as a reaction to events which cost investors billions of dollars. The act's express purpose was ensuring diligent and responsible corporate behavior. It did not take mind-bugs into consideration.

Using Regulations to Prevent Mind-Bugs Generally Creates More Resourceful Mind-Bugs

Jump ahead five years and we find that SOX played no noticeable role in preventing the unsuitably risky corporate behaviors that triggered the global financial crisis. It may even have had the unintended consequence of worsening the 2007 crises. And, many banking and financial services executives justified their poor judgment and behavior, at least to themselves and their boards of directors. This suggests that a more basic problem underlies the recent crises in the oil drilling, automobile, and financial-services industries. If we are looking for a common denominator, we need look no further than mind-bugs.

What Are We Thinking?

Legislators will predictably put in place new rules for financial reform and corporate risk management (along with fines and regulations designed to stop misconduct). But if we want prevention, history suggests that believing regulatory actions will be enough is insanity. Indeed, no matter how noble the intent, the past has demonstrated that well-intentioned reform efforts have led to repeated crises in corporate decision-making. Each new crisis leads to a new bout of poorly crafted and exceedingly complex regulations. The unintended consequence is that corporate governance becomes less viable and the cycle starts over. The logical conclusion is that we must look elsewhere for a solution.

The Problem is Not That We Aren't Thinking, Rather, We Are Not Thinking About Our Thoughts

Solving problems provides a return on investment; solving mere symptoms creates a net loss.[98] When we invest to fix a problem the problem goes away; when we invest in fixing symptoms, they usually return to waste more money. That's what we do when we fail to address mind-bugs; we focus on symptoms instead of the underlying problem. The pervasive presence of mind-bugs regularly results in faulty patterns of thinking and decisions. The only permanent solution is to recognize the artificial sense of security with compliance and become aware of the root cause—mind-bugs. Corporations need to embrace a different way of thinking, or given sufficient time, the results will likely be the same.

Thought Governance

As mentioned in the summary, I believe we need to expand our focus on corporate governance policies to include *thought governance policies*. *"Thought Governance"* implies that we will not take our inherently faulty thinking processes for granted. We will take command of our thinking so it is not in automated control of our decisions. Corporate missions, values, governance, and human resource processes are deficient unless they pay attention to continuous improvement in the quality of individual thinking. Directors need to step up and address this critical omission. Under good *Thought Governance* policies, the responsibility of leadership is to create a culture where mindfulness in decision-making can thrive, to create an organization that is in command of its thinking.

Keeping It Simple

I will say it one more time—this approach will substantially reduce risk. It doesn't require significant investment, burdensome compliance measures, or disproportionate expenditures of time. It is flexible and resilient while designed for accountability and trust. It does, however, require practice and commitment. While losses will still occur, they will less likely be the result of poor judgment, rather, they will reflect the reality that not all risks pay off.

About Competition

Corporations are often more aware of their competition than the quality of their own thinking. Every organization has competitors. Businesses compete for customers, employees, and capital. Cities and states compete to attract new industries, contracts, or government funds. Schools and universities compete for students and faculty. These organizations strive for temporary advantage in a world where "only the strong survive" becomes a condition for continued existence and not merely for competitive advantage. The paradox is that being very good at competing results in ever-increasing competitive intensity and accelerating change. Mind-bugs may cause us to resist change.

The Real Competition

Only when we are in command of our thinking can we realize that however we judge any situation, it is no more than one of many possible perspectives, it is no more than a bundle of thoughts. The still space between stimulus and response is where creativity and solutions are found. But organizations are usually not in this still space. The real competition is between awareness and non-conscious, instinctive response, where the outcome will likely be determined either by the ability of its people to see their own flaws in thinking, or by their corporate stupidity.

Competitive Success

In the next decade and beyond, the ability to collectively advance its quality of thinking will be the single biggest determinant of a company's competitive success. Many of the entrenched management practices that have proven to be so appropriate for the last twenty years, if preserved, may lead to a firm's downfall. The key will be the ability to mindfully challenge and reexamine policies that have served the firm well.

Growing Corporate Awareness

The world today requires that we reevaluate and relearn the way we think, work, and live. I believe the ability of the mind to regularly engage in self-analysis for mind-bugs will increasingly determine the quality of our decisions, our relationships with others, and the joy in our life. When we become aware of the reality of our thinking, we have stepped out of the thousands of years of collective human conditioning and begin to appreciate our mind for what it is.

One World

The world of people and the world of corporations and organizations is one world. A world of mindlessness creates self-serving decisions, defensiveness, justification, blame, and escalating problems. Whereas mindful people invite others to confront their views and readily alter them based on the most complete and valid information possible.

**The path to better decisions lies hidden in plain sight.
It begins with the first step.**

Endnotes

Chapter 0:

1. "Toyota president Akio Toyoda's statement to Congress". The Guardian (London). 2010-02-24. http://www.guardian.co.uk/business/2010/feb/24/akio-toyoda-statement-to-congress.
2. Vlasic, Bill. "Toyota's Slow Awakening to a Deadly Problem" *The New York Times Online* 31 Jan. 2010. A version of this article appeared in print on February 1, 2010, page A1 of the New York edition.
3. Paul, Richard, and Linda Elder. *Critical Thinking: Tools for Taking Charge of Your Professional and Personal Life.* Upper Saddle River, NJ: Financial Times/Prentice Hall, 2002. Print.
4. Easwaran, Eknath. *Words to Live By: a Daily Guide to Leading an Exceptional Life.* Tomales, CA: Nilgiri, 2005. Print.
5. A tip of the hat to authors such as Cipolla, Livraghi, Wells and Pitikin who have written meaningful content on the subject of stupidity.
6. Kleiner, Art. "The Thought Leader Interview: Manfred F.R. Kets De Vries." *Strategy Business: International Business Strategy News Articles and Award-winning Analysis.* 10 May 2010. Web.

Chapter 1:

7. "Debugging Basics: Breakpoints." *MSDN | Microsoft Development, Subscriptions, Resources, and More.* Ed. MIcrosoft. Web. 09 Jan. 2011.
8. Easwaran, Eknath. *Conquest of Mind.* Tomales, CA: Nilgiri, 2001. Print.

Chapter 2:

9. Scientists have determined this number by counting the receptor cells each sense organ has and the nerves that go from these cells to the brain. Wilson, Timothy D. *Strangers to Ourselves: Discovering the Adaptive Unconscious.* Cambridge, MA: Belknap of Harvard UP, 2002. Print.
10. Zimmerman, M. "The Nervous System in the Context of Information Theory." *Human Physiology.* By Robert F. Schmidt and Gerhard Thews. Berlin: Springer-Verlag, 1989. 166-73. Print.

11. Events in the environment can trigger goals and direct our behavior completely outside of conscious awareness. Just as other kinds of thinking can become habitual, automatic, and non-conscious, so can the selection of goals. This adaptive non-conscious is actively involved in learning, selection, interpretation, evaluation, and goal-setting, and the loss of these abilities would be devastating. The fact that non-conscious processes are adaptive does not mean that they always produce error-free judgments. Wilson, Timothy D. *Strangers to Ourselves: Discovering the Adaptive Unconscious.* Cambridge, MA: Belknap of Harvard UP, 2002. Print.

12. There are two main categories of automaticity defined by how the thought or behavior is initiated: Some automatic processes are triggered quite unconsciously, often by stimuli in the environment, whereas others require a conscious act of will to get started. Wheatley, T., and D. M. Wegner. "Automaticity of Action, Psychology of." *International Encyclopedia of the Social & Behavioral Sciences* (2001): 991-93. Print.

13. Wegner, D. M., and J. A. Bargh. "Control and Automaticity in Social Life." *The Handbook of Social Psychology.* By Daniel Todd. Gilbert, Susan T. Fiske, and Gardner Lindzey. 4th ed. Vol. 1. Boston: McGraw-Hill, 1998. 446-96. Print.

14. A behavior is non-conscious if it *resists conscious control*, for example, a person might not be able to stop saying "um" or "you know" despite trying. Uleman, James S., and John A. Bargh. *Unintended Thought.* New York: Guilford, 1989. Print.

15 Langer, Ellen. "Mindful Leadership." NeuroLeadership Summit. Boston USA. 26 Oct. 2010. Lecture.

16. The conscious brain occupies 17 percent of total brain mass while the non-conscious brain occupies 83 percent and controls 96 to 98 percent of perception and behavior. The non-conscious brain has no perception of past or future. The conscious brain operates with a very short-term memory span. Assaraf, John, and Murray Smith. *The Answer: Grow Any Business, Achieve Financial Freedom, and Live an Extraordinary Life.* New York: Atria, 2008. Print.

17. The "fight-or-flight response", also called the "fight-or-flight-or-freeze response", the "fright, fight or flight response", "hyperarousal" or the "acute stress response", was first described by Walter Bradford Cannon in the 1920s. Cannon, M.D. (October 19, 1871–October 1, 1945) was an American physiologist, professor and chairman of the Department of Physiology at Harvard Medical School. He popularized his theories in his book *The Wisdom of the Body.* Cannon, Walter B. *The Wisdom of the Body.* New York: W.W. Norton &, 1939. Print.

18. Baumgarten, David. "How Neuroscientists Seem to Be Using Words and Definitions." E-mail interview. 4 Jan. 2011. Baumgarten is working on a Post Graduate Certificate in the Neuroscience of Leadership as part of pursuing a Masters in the Neuroscience of Leadership.

19. "The mind is not only the site of conscious awareness but also specific psychological capacities such as memory, language, reasoning, perception and emotional responses. Through the mind a person directs their behavior." McHugh, Paul R., and Phillip R. Slavney. The Perspectives of Psychiatry. Baltimore: Johns Hopkins UP, 1998. Print.

20. "The system that started out making sense of all the information bombarding the brain –interpreting our cognitive and emotional responses to what we encounter in our environment – also creates a running narrative of our actions, emotions, thoughts and dreams." Gazzaniga, Michael S. *Human: the Science behind What Makes Us Unique.* New York: Ecco, 2008. Print.

21. Easwaran, Eknath. Conquest of Mind. Tomales, CA: Nilgiri, 2001. Print.

22. Barrett, Lisa Feldman. "A New Model for Emotion & Cognition." NeuroLeadership Summit. Boston USA. 26 Oct. 2010. Lecture.

23. Wilson, Timothy D. *Strangers to Ourselves: Discovering the Adaptive Unconscious.* Cambridge, MA: Belknap of Harvard UP, 2002. Print.

24. Wilson, Timothy D. *Strangers to Ourselves: Discovering the Adaptive Unconscious.* Cambridge, MA: Belknap of Harvard UP, 2002. Print.

Chapter 3:

25. "One of the best studied emotions is fear. If the amygdala recognizes a pattern that was associated with danger in the past, it has a direct shortcut to the brainstem." Gazzaniga, Michael S. Human: the Science behind What Makes Us Unique. New York: Ecco, 2008. Print.

26. "Clearly, we now know much more about how the fear system works. In addition to pinpointing the amygdala as a key structure in the processing of danger, much has been learned about how the amygdala accomplishes its job."LeDoux, Joseph. "The Emotional Brain, Fear, and the Amygdala." *Cellular and Molecular Neurobiology* 23.4/5 (2003): 727-38. Print.

27. "Stress: The Fight or Flight Response." Psychologist World.com. Psychologist World. Web. (The term fight or flight was originated by Walter Cannon in the 1920s as a theory that has been widely studied and adopted.)

28. "After a harmless and aversive stimulus has been encountered, the harmless stimulus on its own will cause fear…including the effects on the hypthalmo-pituitary-adrenal (HPA) axis and sensitization of the fear circuits." Panzar, A., M. Viljoen, and J. L. Roos. "The Neurobiological Basis of Fear: a Concise Review." *South African Psychiatry Review* May (2007): 71-75. Print.

29. "The X-system is a set of neural mechanisms that allow people to see hostility in behavior just as they see size, shape and color in objects. The X-System's operations are fast and automatic and require no conscious attention." Lieberman, M., R. Gaunt, D. Gilbert, and Y. Trope. "Reflexion and Reflection: A Social Cognitive Neuroscience Approach to Attributional Inference." *Advances in Experimental Social Psychology* 34 (2002): 199-249. Print.

30. "Amygdala hijack" is a term coined by Daniel Goleman in his 1996 book *Emotional Intelligence: Why It Can Matter More Than IQ.* Goleman uses the term to describe emotional responses from people which are out of measure with the actual threat because it has triggered a much more significant emotional threat. Goleman, Daniel. *Emotional Intelligence.* New York: Bantam, 2006. Print.

31. Mayo Clinic Staff. "Beyond Shyness: Overcoming the Fear of Social Situations." *Mayo Clinic.* Mayo Foundation for Medical Education and Research, 27 Aug. 2003. Web.

32. Rock, David. "Managing with the Brain in Mind." *Strategy Business: International Business Strategy News Articles and Award-winning Analysis.* Web. 09 Dec. 2008.

33. "Realizing our social status is deeply rooted in our biology not simply our cognition theories about ourselves, we begin to see how the rest of our human equipment helps to guide us through the social maze." Gazzaniga, Michael S. *Human: the Science behind What Makes Us Unique.* New York: Ecco, 2008. Print.

34. Eisenberger, N. I. "Does Rejection Hurt? An FMRI Study of Social Exclusion." *Science* 302.5643 (2003): 290-92. Print.

35. Marmot, M. G. *The Status Syndrome: How Social Standing Affects Our Health and Longevity.* New York: Times, 2004. Print.

36. Brothers, Leslie. *Friday's Footprint: How Society Shapes the Human Mind.* New York: Oxford UP, 1997. Print.

37. Jensen, Eric. *Enriching the Brain: How to Maximize Every Learner's Potential.* San Francisco: Jossey-Bass, 2006. Print.

38. Langer, Ellen J., and Robert P. Abelson. *The Psychology of Control.* Beverly Hills: Sage Publications, 1983. Print.

39. Lieberman, M. D., and N. I. Eisenberger. "NEUROSCIENCE: Pains and Pleasures of Social Life." *Science* 323.5916 (2009): 890-91. Print.

40. McDonald, Paul. "The Potential Contribution of Neuroscience to Authentic Leadership." *NeuroLeadership Journal* Issue Two (2009): 53-66. Print.

41. Van Den Bos, Kees, and Joost Miedema. "Toward Understanding Why Fairness Matters: The Influence of Mortality Salience on Reactions to Procedural Fairness." *Journal of Personality and Social Psychology* 79.3 (2000): 355-66. Print.
42. Jensen, Eric. *Brain-based Learning: the New Paradigm of Teaching.* Thousand Oaks, CA.: Corwin, 2008. Print.

Chapter 4:
43. In *Influence,* Robert Cialdini's book about social psychology and influence tactics, Cialdini explains how common automatic response patterns are in human behavior, and how easily they can be triggered, even with erroneous cues. Cialdini, Robert B. *Influence: the Psychology of Persuasion.* New York: Collins, 2007. Print.
44. Baumgarten, David. "How Neuroscientists Seem to Be Using Words and Definitions." E-mail interview. 4 Jan. 2011. Baumgarten is working on a Post Graduate Certificate in the Neuroscience of Leadership as part of pursuing a Masters in the Neuroscience of Leadership.
45. Paul, Richard, and Linda Elder. *Critical Thinking: Tools for Taking Charge of Your Professional and Personal Life.* Upper Saddle River, NJ: Financial Times/Prentice Hall, 2002. Print.
46. Kim, Jaegwon. "Thought." *Wikipedia, the Free Encyclopedia.* Web. 10 Jan. 2011. <http://en.wikipedia.org/wiki/Thought>. Honderich, Ted. *The Oxford Companion to Philosophy.* Oxford: Oxford UP, 1995. Print.
47. "The way we think is not the way we think we think." Fauconnier, Gilles, and Mark Turner. *The Way We Think: Conceptual Blending and the Mind's Hidden Complexities.* New York: Basic, 2002. Print.
48. Cornelius, Randolph R. *The Science of Emotion: Research and Tradition in the Psychology of Emotions.* Upper Saddle River, NJ: Prentice Hall, 1996. Print.
49. Barrett, Lisa Feldman. "A New Model for Emotion & Cognition." NeuroLeadership Summit. Boston USA. 26 Oct. 2010. Lecture.

Chapter 5:
50. Langer, Ellen J. *Mindfulness.* Reading, MA: Addison-Wesley Pub., 1989. Print.
51. Lieberman, M., R. Gaunt, D. Gilbert, and Y. Trope. "Reflexion and Reflection: A Social Cognitive Neuroscience Approach to Attributional Inference." *Advances in Experimental Social Psychology* 34 (2002): 199-249. Print.
52. "Non-reflective beliefs are fast and automatic. It is as if we are not yet comfortable with our rational, analytical mind. In terms of evolution, it is a new ability that we humans have recently come upon, and we appear to use it sparingly." Gazzaniga, Michael S. *Human: the Science behind What Makes Us Unique.* New York: Ecco, 2008. Print.

Chapter 6:
53. "…brain scientist Jeffrey Schwartz and I proposed that organizations could marshal mindful attention to create organizational change. They could do this over time by putting in place regular routines in which people would watch the patterns of their thoughts and feelings as they worked and thus develop greater self-awareness…" David Rock "The Neuroscience of Leadership." *Strategy Business: International Business Strategy News Articles and Award-winning Analysis.* 30 May 2006. Web.
54. Easwaran, Eknath. *Words to Live By: a Daily Guide to Leading an Exceptional Life.* Tomales, CA: Nilgiri, 2005. Print.
55. "Is it the actual truth, or is it one that verifies how you see the world, or one that maintains your status and reputation? We have to have enough time to think about it so the automatic response doesn't kick in. Research has shown that people will use the first argument that satisfies their opinion and then stop thinking." Gazzaniga, Michael S. Human: the Science behind What Makes Us Unique. New York: Ecco, 2008. Print.

Chapter 10:

56. "Everything you do in life is determined by the quality of your thinking." Paul, Richard, and Linda Elder. *Critical Thinking: Tools for Taking Charge of Your Professional and Personal Life*. Upper Saddle River, NJ: Financial Times/Prentice Hall, 2002. Print.

57. "Trying to drink from a fire hose of information has harmful effects. And nowhere are those effects clearer, and more worrying, than in our ability to make smart, creative successful decisions" Begley, Sharon. "I Can't Think." *Newsweek* 7 Mar. 2011. Print.

58. "We are often diverted from rationality by our need to think well of ourselves, getting entangled in a quagmire of defensiveness." Anderson, Barry F. *The Three Secrets of Wise Decision Making*. Portland, OR: Single Reef, 2002. Print.

59. Lovallo, Dan, and Olivier Sibony. "A Language to Discuss Biases." *Articles by McKinsey Quarterly: Online Business Journal of McKinsey & Company*. McKinsey & Company, Apr. 2010. Web.

Chapter 11:

60. "Another way that we become mindless is by forming a mindset when we first encounter something and then cling to it when we reencounter that same thing. Because such mindsets form before we do much reflection, we call them premature cognitive commitments. When we accept an impression or a piece of information at face value, that impression settles unobtrusively into our minds." Langer, Ellen J. *Mindfulness*. Reading, MA: Addison-Wesley Pub., 1989. Print.

Chapter 12:

61. In the 1920s, Mary Parker Follett, a pioneer in management studies, anticipated certain of these ideas. Follett's warnings about an obsession with outcome are pertinent for any manager today: "A system built round a purpose is dead before it is born. Purpose unfolds and reflects the means." Follett, Mary Parker., Henry C. Metcalf, and L. Urwick. *Dynamic Administration: The Collected Papers of Mary Parker Follett*. London: Taylor & Francis, 2003. Print.

62. "We are likely to say, if asked, that the decision to act produced the actions themselves. Recent discoveries, however, challenge this causal status of conscious will. They demonstrate that under some conditions, actions are initiated even though we are unconscious of the goals to be attained or their motivating effect on our behavior." Custers, Ruud, and Henk Aarts. "The Unconscious Will: How the Pursuit of Goals Operates Outside of Conscious Awareness." *Science*. American Association for the Advancement of Science, 1 July 2010. Web.

63. McKinsey's Olivier Sibony asked Dan Ariely (author of Predictably Irrational); "What distinguishes a situation when an executive should trust his intuition or his gut feeling, versus one where he should really pause and think?" Ariely advised there are conditions when we have plenty of experience and we have unambiguous feedback. However, the moment a random component is added, performance goes away very quickly. And the world in which executives live in is a world with lots of random elements. Ariely, Dan, and Olivier Sibony. "Dan Ariely on Irrationality in the Workplace." *McKinsey Quarterly* (2011). Print.

64. Bargh studied the way people select information for further processing from the vast amount available. It was found that self-relevant information required fewer attentional resources. Bargh, John A. "Attention and Automaticity in the Processing of Self-relevant Information." *Journal of Personality and Social Psychology* 43.3 (1982): 425-36. Print.

Chapter 13:

65. This classic of social psychology is based on the idea that people in groups might think differently and by implication less well than they would have thought as individuals on the same issue at the same time. Janis, Irving L. *Groupthink: Psychological Studies of Policy Decisions and Fiascoes*. Boston: Houghton Mifflin, 1982. Print.

66. "The C-suite displays a consistently "rose-tinted" view of engagement that is not shared lower down the ranks. One important revelation from our survey is the huge disparity between the views of many in the C-suite and those of less senior directors, including just a single rung below board level. For example, 47% of C-suite executives believe that they themselves have determined levels of employee engagement, a view shared by only 16% of senior directors outside the C-suite. Hay Group." Re-engaging with Engagement." *Business Research*. Web. 2010.

67. A good example of this appears in a recent Hay Survey. "A significant mismatch exists between words and deeds on engagement. There are clear inconsistencies in our survey findings, which suggest that words come more easily than concrete actions. For example, 84% of survey respondents say that "disengaged employees" are one of the three biggest threats facing their business. Yet it appears that little is done to identify, support or even "weed out" unengaged staff." Hay Group. "Re-engaging with Engagement." *Business Research*. 2010. Web.

Chapter 15:

68. See Chapter Two, beginning on page 33.

69. "When we are intentionally attentive, we are being purposeful. We are purposely open to new information. Attention is a resource and a potential way to generate value to ourselves and others. As with all resources, attention is limited individually and collectively within organizations." Yeganeh, Bauback. *Mindful Experiential Learning*. Diss. Case Western Reserve University, 2006. Print.

70. Kabat-Zinn, John. "Mindfulness-based Interventions in Context: Past, Present, and Future." *Clinical Psychology: Science and Practice* 10 (2003): 144-56. Print.

71. See Chapter 2, beginning on page 33 – No Help from Our Brain – Brain Signals

72. "Understanding the powerful role of emotions in the workplace sets the best leaders apart from the rest –not just in tangibles such as better business results and the retention of talent, but also the intangibles such as higher morale, motivation, and commitment." Goleman, Daniel, Richard E. Boyatzis, and Annie McKee. *Primal Leadership: Realizing the Power of Emotional Intelligence*. Boston, MA: Harvard Business School, 2002. Print.

73. "The fascinating thing is that these feelings come from the brain itself and its perceptions as to what is happening to us and how we like those things. The feelings then are both created and perceived by the brain. They directly influence our behaviors and attitudes." Zull, James E. *The Art of Changing the Brain: Enriching Teaching by Exploring the Biology of Learning*. Sterling, VA: Stylus Pub., 2002. Print.

74. Baddeley's model integrates a large amount of findings from work on short-term and working memory. Additionally, the mechanisms have inspired a wealth of research in experimental psychology, neuropsychology, and cognitive neuroscience. Baddeley, Alan D. *Working Memory*. Oxford, Oxfordshire: Clarendon, 1986. Print.

75. Kennedy, Alan, and Alan Wilkes. *Studies in Long Term Memory*. London: Wiley, 1975. Print: 3-18 Broadbent, D.E. (1975), The Magic Number Seven after Fifteen Years.

76. Microsoft is also aware that individuals are terrible at understanding their own patterns. "The information that they provide rarely aligns with the data produced when studying humans with GPS devices and sensors." Kanellos, Michael. "Video: Microsoft Attempts to Predict the Future. Epicenter. Wired.com." *Wired.com*. Conde Nast Digital, 10 May 2010. Web.

77. This was first brought to the author's attention when working on a project with The Arbinger Institute. *Leadership and Self-deception: Getting out of the Box*. San Francisco, CA: Berrett-Koehler, 2002. Print.

78. "Amygdala hijack" is a term coined by Daniel Goleman using the term to describe emotional responses from people which are out of measure with the actual threat. Goleman, Daniel. *Emotional Intelligence*. New York: Bantam, 2006. Print.

Chapter 16:

79. Braza, Jerry. *Moment by Moment: the Art and Practice of Mindfulness*. Boston: C.E. Tuttle, 1997. Print.

80. The best overall test for irrationality [mind-bugs] is the response to challenging information. "There's no sense in talking about it anymore!" "I've been through all that, and it's just not worth our spending any more time on!" "Don't be silly!" "I don't want to talk about it!" "We don't do things that way around here!" "I can see right now that that won't work!" "I don't want any experiments!" "There's really no other alternative!" "I find this whole discussion upsetting!" Anderson, Barry F. *The Three Secrets of Wise Decision Making*. Portland, OR: Single Reef, 2002. Print.

81. Kabat-Zinn, Jon. *Wherever You Go, There You Are: Mindfulness Meditation in Everyday Life*. New York: Hyperion, 1994. Print.

82. Yarbus, A. L. *Eye Movements and Vision,*. New York: Plenum, 1967. Print.

83. "While mindfulness is clearly a state of being, individuals differ in their propensity or willingness to be aware and to sustain attention to what is occurring in the present and this mindful capacity varies within persons, because it can be sharpened or dulled by a variety of factors." Brown, K. W., and R. M. Ryan. "The Benefits of Being Present: Mindfulness and Its Role in Psychological Well Being." *Journal of Personality and Social Psychology* 84 (2003): 822-48. Print.

84. "Breakpoints allow software programmers to control execution of the program and specify how and where the application will stop to allow further examination for bugs." Rosenberg, Jonathan B. *How Debuggers Work: Algorithms, Data Structures, and Architecture*. New York: John Wiley, 1996. Print.

85. Mindfulness can be stimulated "when familiar situations require more effortful processing, when situational factors disrupt the initiation or completion of automatic routines, and when consequences differ substantially from expectations." Bodner, T., and E. Langer. *Individual Differences in Mindfulness: The Langer Mindfulness Scale. Poster Session Presented at the Annual Meeting of the American Psychological Society, Toronto, Ont., Canada*. 2001. Print.

86. After identifying five basic assumptions concerning the relationship between psychological stress and decisional conflict, five distinct patterns including defensive avoidance emerge. Janis, Irving L., and Leon Mann. *Decision Making: a Psychological Analysis of Conflict, Choice, and Commitment*. New York: Free, 1977. Print.

Chapter 17:

87. This survey is intentionally worded negatively measuring mindlessness rather than mindfulness. "Statements reflecting less mindlessness are likely more accessible to most individuals, given that mindless states are much more common than mindful states". Indirect claims may be more "diagnostic" than direct claims to mindfulness. Brown, Kirk Warren, and Richard M. Ryan. "Perils and Promise in Defining and Measuring Mindfulness: Observations From Experience." *Clinical Psychology: Science and Practice* September 11.3 (2004): 242-48. Print.

88. "Starting from the obvious fact that professional intuition is sometimes marvelous and sometimes flawed; the authors attempt to map the boundary conditions that separate true intuitive skill from overconfident and biased impressions. They conclude that evaluating the likely quality of an intuitive judgment requires an assessment of the predictability of the environment in which the judgment is made and of the individual's opportunity to learn the regularities of that environment. Subjective experience is not a reliable indicator of judgment accuracy (ResearchGate)." Kahneman, Daniel, and Gary Klein. "Conditions for Intuitive Expertise: A Failure to Disagree." *American Psychologist* 64.6 (2009): 515-26. Print.

Chapter 18:

89. This is similar to the problem of an infinite loop in computer programs. An infinite loop is a sequence of instructions in a computer program which loops endlessly, either

due to the loop having no terminating condition, having one that can never be met, or one that causes the loop to start over. Most often, the term is used for those situations when this is not the intended result; that is, when this is a bug. A mind-bug spiral can also loop endlessly. "Infinite Loop." *Wikipedia, the Free Encyclopedia*. 2 May 2011. Web. <http://en.wikipedia.org/wiki/Infinite_loop>.

90. Easwaran, Eknath. *Conquest of Mind*. Tomales, CA: Nilgiri, 2001. Print.

Chapter 19:

91. Argyris, Chris. *Reasons and Rationalizations the Limits to Organizational Knowledge*. Oxford: Oxford UP, 2006. Print.

Chapter 22:

92. "Because good thinking is so important and so difficult, we rightly hold in high regard those who become proficient at it. The best we call wise". Anderson, Barry F. *The Three Secrets of Wise Decision Making*. Portland, OR: Single Reef, 2002. Print.

93. Chinese proverb and favorite quote of Justin Stone, originator of T'ai Chi Chih.

Chapter 23:

94. "Research by Mitchell, Deborah J. (Wharton), J. Edward Russo (Cornell), and Nancy Pennington (University of Colorado) found that prospective hindsight—imagining that an event has already occurred—increases the ability to correctly identify reasons for future outcomes by 30%.". Klein, Gary. "Performing a Project Premortem - Harvard Business Review." *Harvard Business Review Case Studies, Articles, Books*. Harvard Business Publishing, Sept. 2007. Web.

95. "Some automatic processes do not require any willful initiation and operate quite independently of conscious control. These processes can be instigated by stimuli of which we are not yet conscious, or by stimuli of which we were recently conscious but are no longer." Bargh, John A., Mark Chen, and Lara Burrows. "Automaticity of Social Behavior: Direct Effects of Trait Construct and Stereotype Activation on Action." *Journal of Personality and Social Psychology* 71.2 (1996): 230-44. Print.

96. "Most of our thoughts and behaviors tend to be automatic. And, we may find under conditions of mental load or stress that the automatic processes that occur to monitor the failure of our conscious intentions ironically create that failure." Wheatley, T., and D. M. Wegner. "Automaticity of Action, Psychology of." *International Encyclopedia of the Social & Behavioral Sciences* (2001): 991-93. Print.

97. "Debuggers are the magnifying glass, the microscope, the logic analyzer, the profiler, and the browser with which a program can be examined." Rosenberg, Jonathan B. *How Debuggers Work: Algorithms, Data Structures, and Architecture*. New York: John Wiley, 1996. Print.

Chapter 27:

98. Jensen, Eric. *Enriching the Brain: How to Maximize Every Learner's Potential*. San Francisco: Jossey-Bass, 2006. Print.

Acknowledgements and Gratitude

Team Mind-Bugs

I've got a fever***
and the only prescription is to eliminate mind-bugs

ı ı ı ı ı ∎ ∎ ∎ ∎ ∎ ∎ ∎ ∎ ∎ ı ı ı ı ı

Acknowledgements to...

○ the human race for being such a beautiful mess. Just like me, there are millions of people on this planet who despite having the potential to know better, continue to choose worse and make flawed decisions. We have been the inspiration that made the writing of this book a very serious and personally meaningful undertaking.

❂ the scientists, academics, authors, and practitioners in many fields who research and write about flaws in human thinking. You continue

---

*** Influenced by "More cowbell", an American pop culture catchphrase originally derived from an April 8, 2000, Saturday Night Live comedy sketch. Thanks to Will Ferrell, Jimmy Fallon, Christopher Walken "The Bruce Dickinson", and Blue Öyster Cult for the SNL skit. You encouraged me to "really explore the space".

to provide a credible and exciting foundation upon which to explore, learn, and grow.

- ❃ my dad, Aaron Bloom, whose simple daily message growing up of "show EJ" continues to inspire me to show Excellent Judgment. I wish it were that simple.
- ✰ Nan O'Connor, who worked with me during an important development stage of this book. She asked amazingly helpful questions and made important suggestions as the book took a life of its own. At one time we were planning to co-author. As it turned out, we thought we were directing our lives but found our lives were directing us.
- ❦ my wife Yvonne, for the numerous private conversations about my research, along with her counseling, encouragement, criticisms, and unwavering love despite my own stupidity. And, thanks for coming up with the term *mind-bugs* to describe it all. Bzzzzz!
- ➲ my son Adam, for his critiques, challenges, and feedback on the manuscript drafts and references. Also high fives for your direct work on the social media, marketing, and web development, along with joining me on a quest to help contribute to a brighter planet by reducing mind-bugs.
- ✪ the rest of my family. Mom, Amanda, and Max for your loving support and encouragement, and my dog Bella, who was at my side most of the last 5 years of research and likely wonders why humans mumble to themselves so much.
- ◗ my dear friend David Baumgarten, who runs a private business while pursuing his masters in NeuroLeadership. Through fourteen rounds, his feedback, critique, and suggestions on Figure 2-2 made a significant contribution to this body of work. THANK YOU!
- ❁ all of my old and new friends who acted as sounding boards. Your overwhelming amount of connectivity to the terms Corporate Stupidity and Mind-Bugs was extremely motivational. Also a special thanks to Rod Sterling who reflected with me early on: how big does a company need to be before it becomes stupid?

✌ my editors and book project managers at Höhne-Werner Design. Angela Werner and Michael Höhne combined years of experience and a thorough understanding of the process with their own passion for the book to help me create a finished product that can make a difference in the world. Their knowhow, patience, discipline, and willingness to explore their own mind-bugs were exactly what I needed, along with more commas and more cowbell. I highly recommend them to other authors.   http://www.heyneon.com

Appendices

A. Steps, Tools, and Practices
B. How the Book Wrote Itself
C. The Research
D. References

The Steps, Tools, and Practices

Honoring those who have decided this book is useful and intend to use it, I have organized many of the "tools" in one place. I want to provide everything you need to "jump to quickly" as a reminder of the actual processes, practices, and steps. Each item references the source chapter/page to make it easy to navigate. It also tells a story on its own to the busy reader.

Step, Tool, or Practice	Source Chapter/Page
1. Mind-Bugs and Dimensions	Ch. 8/70 & 71
2. Sufficiency Dimension Mind-Bugs	Ch. 9/74
3. Accuracy Dimension Mind-Bugs	Ch. 9/75
4. Beliefs Dimension Mind-Bugs	Ch. 9/76
5. Social Dimension Mind-Bugs	Ch. 9/77
6. The Six Step Path to Better Decisions	Ch. 16/110 Ch. 25/158
7. The Six Steps, Tools, and Practices	Ch. 25/159
8. The Two Ways	Ch. 5/55
9. The Two Questions	Ch. 18/120
10. Group Debugging	Ch. 19/129
11. The 30 Second Scan	Ch. 22/146
12. The Debugging Process	Ch. 23/149

Figure 8-1

Mind-Bugs and Dimensions

Dimensions			
Sufficiency	Accuracy	Beliefs	Social
Informed Leader Fallacy	Unverified Information vs. Fact	Outcome Attachment	Conforming Error
Source Influence	Generalization without Evidence	Shortcomings Denial	Rose-colored Glasses
Assumption Error	Seeing Patterns that are not real	Closed Mind	Power Insulation
Snap Judgment Defense	Data Rejection	Experience Bias	Status Quo
Shooting the Critics	Data Favoritism	Competency Blindness	Hiding Weakness

Business decisions are generally based on verified information communicated from a point of view within a social context.

Figure 8-2

The Four Dimensions of Mind-Bugs

Dimensions			
Sufficiency	Accuracy	Beliefs	Social
Mind-Bugs in these dimensions lead to errors in the way we gather information		Mind-Bugs in these dimensions lead to errors in the way we process information	
Do I have the correct inputs?	Are the inputs truthful?	How do I color my decision process?	What is the influence of others?

The way we gather information affects what we process and the way we process information affects what we gather. Mind-bugs cause flaws in these fundamental decision-making activities and have an impact across the four dimensions.

Table 9-1

The Sufficiency Dimension Mind-Bugs	
The requirement to make decisions based on both relevant and significant information of adequate breadth and depth.	
Informed Leader Fallacy	A belief by a leader that he/she is better informed and has better instincts than others, simply because he/she is the leader.
Example: A high level manager decides to fire an employee without seeking the advice of others because he believes he is well-informed. After the fact, he learns things about the employee's performance that indicate his was a poor decision.	
Source Influence	Determining level of sufficiency depending on the source.
Example: When our boss suggests something, we may subconsciously accept it as complete without any challenge. When someone we are competing with suggests something, we may seek to find fault.	
Assumption Error	Basing decisions on assumptions we believe are true, without challenging those assumptions.
Example: A CEO assumes his company can design a component better than purchasing an existing component from outside the company. Result, spending money on R&D when a good solution already exists.	
Snap Judgment Defense	Defending decisions made solely on snap judgment.
Example: Due to the high pressure atmosphere at work, a manager makes a snap judgment to move an employee from one position to another and informs the employee of the change. When another manager questions this move, the decision-maker becomes defensive and incapable of hearing another perspective.	
Shooting the Critics	The tendency to marginalize people who disagree with us.
Example: The head of quality at a large manufacturer hires an employee who comes with new ideas and a desire to express them. Sometimes this employee disagrees with his boss. Over time, the boss quits inviting him to key meetings and eventually he is completely out of the decision loop.	

Table 9-2

The Accuracy Dimension Mind-Bugs	
The requirement to make decisions based on information that is clearly defined, reliable, factual, precise, and fair.	
Unverified Information vs. Fact	Causes us to confuse unverified information with facts.
Example: I want to drop the price of our product A to generate more sales this month. I trust that three of my experienced colleagues believe that doing this is a good idea (unverified information). However, a customer survey would provide facts that show customer inventory is already too high and no sales increase would occur (Fact). If I fail to examine my mind-bugs, I will drop prices on unverified information, rather than fact.	
Generalization without Evidence	Making generalizations without the evidence to back them up.
Example: The profit margin on product A has maintained a steady 35% for two years. Is that sufficient to project that margin will be 35% for the next five years? No, not based solely on this information.	
Seeing Patterns that are not Real	Seeing patterns in random data when none exist.
Example: Since customers have not complained about the quality of our new product we must not have any problems.	
Data Rejection	A reflex-like rejection of new facts because they contradict existing norms.
Example: A fortune 500 company appointed its public relations department to organize all the divisional websites to harmonize with the corporate site. Businesses with different needs had their sites rejected without consideration—chaos broke out.	
Data Favoritism	Selecting, using and favoring data in a self-serving, unquestioning way.
Example: One study suggests that Product A performs at 2 ounces per gallon. Another study, of equal quality, concludes that Product A performs at 5 ounces per gallon. I want to beat competition, so I use the data from the first survey without determining why differing results occurred.	

Table 9-3

The Beliefs Dimension Mind-Bugs	
The requirement to consider the influence of one's own perspective, desires, values, and emotions in conjunction with any decision.	
Outcome Attachment	Being so attached to outcomes that serve our interest that we fail to look for problems in our thinking and decisions.
Example: A CEO knows that her job depends on hitting next year's numbers. When there is an opportunity to sandbag revenue from this year and put it into next year, she decides to do it without examining the consequences.	
Shortcomings Denial	Underestimating our own shortcomings by not knowing or believing we have them or rationalizing and assuming we can control them.
Example: When Bob receives a promotion to Director of Sales, his boss suggests he hire an assistant to help pay attention to the details. Bob knows that he is not a detail person, but decides against the assistant. He believes that because he is aware of his shortcoming he will overcome it.	
Closed Mind	The inability to hold and examine two opposing views at the same time and to be closed to other perspectives than our own.
Example: I am convinced that the new product we have been investing in for the last 18 months will be successful. When our head of marketing expresses concerns about the product, I pay lip service to her concerns and then continue with the product launch, as is.	
Experience Bias	Believing that future events will occur in a specific way, based on prior experience—not realizing that past experience is not always predictive of future reality.
Example: If I have lead a successful product launch in the past I may believe that the conditions and decisions of the next product launch will be similar. If my belief is strong I fail to look for contradictory evidence and make a higher-risk decision.	
Competency Blindness	Believing others are competent in areas when they are not and vice versa when it suits our subconscious needs.
Example: My right-hand person has always delivered. No matter what I have asked him to do, he has taken on the challenge and come through with flying colors. I decide to have him tackle a problem we are having with quality control. He fails miserably. I did not consider whether he was competent in that particular expertise.	

Table 9-4

The Social Dimension Mind-Bugs	
Consideration of the influence of the group's definition of reality along with bureaucracy, power structure, and vested interests, in conjunction with decisions.	
Conforming Error	Subconsciously conforming our thinking to the thinking of our group.
Example: When Bob first joined the company, he couldn't believe the inefficiencies that existed in the billing process. But, everyone said that this is just the way things are in their industry. Over time, Bob has come to believe them.	
Rose-colored Glasses	Overestimating the likelihood of positive events because everyone in the group believes they will happen.
Example: A special task force has been in place for the launch of a new product. They have worked hard for the past six months to get the product to market. They feel so good about the product that they promise a certain level of revenue in the first year without data to back up their projections.	
Power Insulation	The power structure of a group discourages disturbances to their beliefs.
Example: A consultant is brought in to help a group with strategic planning. He quickly realizes that they are not achieving the kind of margins that are possible. When he challenges them, he is told that he simply doesn't understand because their business is different. The management team refuses to objectively evaluate his recommendations.	
Status Quo	Sticking to the status quo and creating significant friction that works against new ideas.
Example: Your company is considering introducing digital machinery on the shop floor. Several foremen point out the many ways that the learning curve will seriously slow down current production and quality, ignoring the large benefits of increased quality and production once the transition period is over.	
Hiding Weaknesses	The tendency to hide our weaknesses by presenting the most favorable picture to outsiders.
Example: A partner company is brought in to develop software that will analyze project management efficiency. The partner is not told up front that there is deep internal disagreement as to the accuracy of the data on which the software will be based.	

Figure 25-1

The Six Step Path to Better Decisions Ratio

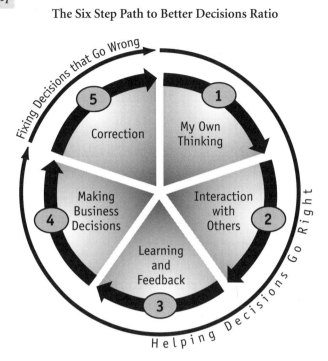

This implies that 80% of leadership, management, supervisor, team leader, and employee time should be spent helping make good decisions and only 20% of their time in fixing bad decisions. All too often this ratio gets reversed in corporations. To discover the reason we must look below the surface of our problems, at mind-bugs. Figure 25-2 on the next page lays out the tools and practices for each step.

Figure 25-2

Steps, Tools, and Practices*

Step	Description	Tools and Practices
1	Practice mindfulness in my own thinking	§ Read this book § MBA Index and Advanced MBA Index § The Two Questions § Mind-Bugs Reference Chart
2	Practice mindful interaction with others	§ Everyone reads and discusses this book § MBA Index and Advanced MBA Index § The Two Questions § Mind-Bugs Reference Chart
3	Practice mindfulness in learning and feedback	§ The Learning Awareness Index (LA Index) § The Two Questions
4	Make mindful decisions	§ 30 second scan § Decision Debugging Process
5	Be mindful in the way I take and give correction	§ The Six Steps § The Two Questions
6	Mindfully begin again at step one	§ Review the book § Use The Two Questions § Check progress and make corrections

Figure 5-1

The Two Ways to Do Everything

The Two Ways:	My behavior is:	I am:	Mind-Bugs:
1. I am in command of my thoughts	Reflective	Mindful	Avoided
2. My thoughts are in command of me	Reactive	Mindless	Thrive

The Two Questions

You can ask two questions about anything in life and receive benefit because they provide a mental breakpoint to promote mindfulness, which is being in command of our thinking.

The two questions work best when asked as early as possible in a project, meeting, relationship, decision, contemplated action, etc. But it is never too late to benefit. Merely questioning ourselves about The Two Ways helps to identify and avoid mind-bugs.

Tool: Group De-bugging

Meet with a group of people with whom you are working to deliver results. Identify a specific result you are working to deliver together. Distribute individual copies of the Mind-Bug Reference Chart. As it relates to the specific result:

1. Have each person identify the top three mind-bugs where each believes they are personally most vulnerable as it relates to this result.

2. Have each person identify the top three mind-bugs where each believes the group is most vulnerable.

3. Discuss the mind-bugs as a group.

4. Identify how the mind-bugs could cause problems.

5. Identify how to avoid problems and help decisions go right.

6. Have fun with the discussions.

Tool: The 30 Second Decision Scan

For each decision we are about to make simply answer yes or no to the following.

Have we sufficiently considered …

1. … how the personal stake or vested interest for each person or group involved could influence this evaluation?

2. … how beliefs and desires may have colored or influenced any judgments or inferences?

3. … if there are any critical gaps in the sufficiency of the information used to support our arguments?

4. … what makes us confident that the data we are depending on is accurate?

5. … what mind-bugs may be present that could affect our judgment?

6. … if I should continue with this decision if my answer is no to any of the first five questions?

You will soon see that if the answer to question 6 is "no," then you are exposed to mind-bugs.

Tool: The Debugging Process

Here are the steps in the basic Mind-Bug Debugging process.

1. Insert mental breakpoints in the decision process.

   a. The team intentionally pauses to examine the current state of the decision.
   b. Everyone adopts an attitude that they are willing to investigate viewpoints that differ from their own with the goal of getting at the truth.

2. Clarify and agree on the decision construct to be used for debugging as follows:

   a. What is the basic purpose of the decision?
   b. What are the conclusions that support this decision?
   c. What assumptions are you using to support each conclusion?
   d. What information are you using to support either the assumptions or conclusions directly?

3. Inspect and evaluate each conclusion one at a time along with the related assumptions, information, and any other reasoning.

   a. Using the mind-bug list, each team member identifies the mind-bugs they sense each conclusion is most susceptible to.
   b. The results are compiled by identifying the top 3-5 mind-bugs associated with each conclusion and sharing with the team.

4. Debug

   a. The team discusses the merits of each and how they can be avoided.
   b. The team discusses what important evidence may have been omitted or suppressed due to mind-bugs.
   c. The team determines if it should revise any of the arguments and how it will avoid mind-bugs.

5. Depending on the complexity and timeline, future breakpoints are established at preset conditions to insure new infection does not occur as the decision state changes.

Appendix B: How the Book Wrote Itself

Understanding the problem, doing the research, and keeping it simple.

Have you ever noticed a bad decision being made and asked, "What the heck are they thinking?" Perhaps you thought to yourself; "that's a stupid idea", but you didn't tell anyone that could have influence. Or, maybe you looked back at a bad decision of your own and justified it by saying, "Well, it seemed like a good idea at the time." If you have, then you understand what drove the writing and research for this book. It started with the realization that a problem I was experiencing at work was due to a fault occurring in the space between my own ears. Although I did not use the term at that time, I had a mind-bug.

Team Mind-Bugs Feels Your Pain

Over the years I collaborated with many others regarding various aspects of my findings; some of those conversations pointed me down new roads and I am thankful for the many inputs along the way. Although it is not formalized, I enjoy referring to this group as "team mind-bugs." So, while the writing is mine, there were many "we"s along the way. And, we feel your pain.

Hands on Experience

This book brings a personal experience and perspective very different from the highly regarded PhD researchers at academic institutions. My approach was first to gain insight into how internal human factors cause bad decisions to occur. Next, I leveraged significant real-world hands-on experience with over four years of secondary research, taking advantage of the excellent body of information that exists across many disciplines. Then I developed a simple, practical, and useful model to illuminate how faulty decisions might be avoided in cases where people could have known better, chose worse, and thus caused harm.

Keeping it Real

The book and model were conceived based on a clear understanding that people in corporations are extremely busy. The book is not burdened with in-text references or citations. It is intended to be something you can easily read and try on to see for yourself if you find any value. You can put it aside and try it again in the future without harming the learning process. Insightful footnotes are provided for the reader who wants to know more, but reading them is optional. The book is quite intentionally not a scientific paper and is not intended for publication as such.

Solid Research-Driven Concepts

While somewhat unique in its simple approach and use of metaphors like mind-bugs to address complex problems, the concepts are grounded in primary and secondary research and I sense that a social psychologist, neuroscientist, or other category expert would find the material does not miss the mark. To make it easy for someone who wants to dive deeper, the six underlying scientific themes of the book are laid out and supported with specific references and abstracts of each in Appendix C. Appendix D provides an extensive list of references. I honor those whose research contributed to my own thinking. If you just need to know there is a scientific basis for this work, then reading the abstracts should provide sufficient support. If you are a research junkie, then you will certainly enjoy reading some of these works.

The Research —
Mind-Bugs Fundamental Themes

An Introduction to the Supporting Research

The impetus for the research for this book originated many years ago. Since my realization that I had a problem with my own thinking, I've explored hundreds of books, articles, and research papers as I continued to learn and grow. My job became an informal laboratory and later so did the relationships with other professionals, my family, and my friends.

The Building Blocks

The research spanned many different disciplines. After digesting scores of facts, ideas, procedures, methods, concepts, principles, hypotheses, and discoveries, and comparing them to my own real life experiences, I observed a set of five fundamental themes that regularly appeared across diverse areas of specialized research and theory. These themes are the elemental building blocks for the mind-bugs model.

1. Scientists simply do not yet know how the brain generates the mind. But, the human organ, the physical object, the grey matter that is called the brain, is intimately connected to the feelings, desires, and decisions that occur in our mind. They are not the same and yet they are not separate.

2. As humans, we are hard-wired for survival and programmed to react to threats. Fear is a universal biological emotion generated by the human brain when it perceives a threat. It is an automatic response to the internally-processed perception of the threat, not to the threat itself. It is critical to survival and is a fundamental part of being human. What is brilliant from a primitive survival standpoint can cause significant problems in other situations. As a result, we have a non-conscious predisposition for irrationality.

3. When triggered by a survival reaction, the processes of our brain take priority over those of our mind, resulting in unexamined thoughts, feelings, desires, and decisions. Over time, the conse–quence can be an accumulation of faulty beliefs, biased judgments, mistakes of reason, and compulsive habits of thinking. Once these have entered our mind, it is difficult to turn them off.

4. Faulty decisions can occur when our attachment to our thoughts, feelings, desires, and decisions are stronger than our ability to let go of those attachments easily. These "attachments of the mind" present themselves in many ways. For the purpose of our model I call them mind-bugs.

5. When we are not mindful of our thoughts, we *react* without even being aware that we are reacting. An interruption is required, or the automatic responses kick in and stay until the perceived threat is gone and cortisol has left the brain. This "mental breakpoint" requires a higher level of self-awareness.

Making it Easy to Understand the Research

I am not a scientist in the field; I am merely adapting the existing sig-nificant body of research to create a simple-to-understand model that is practical for use in organizations. To make it easy for interested parties to learn more about some of the underlying research, I have selected one or more books or papers in each of many fields of expertise and then provided a brief summary for each. The summaries identify the author and credentials, and then attempt to briefly correlate the mind-bug themes. Of course, each document contains more references, leading to thousands of pages of data that can be accessed.

The selection of sources is not intended to be comprehensive nor are the fields of research completely represented. Rather the goal is merely to give the reader an easy-to-digest taste of the underlying research. A more complete list of references is also provided for folks who wish to read even further. I am very grateful to all those who are researching, connecting, and writing about these themes. Someone must do the basic research so that others can look across the work in an attempt to draw practical insight.

Twelve Fields of Research and Correlated Abstracts

1. Psychiatry

McHugh, Paul R., and Phillip R. Slavney. *The Perspectives of Psychiatry.* Baltimore: Johns Hopkins UP, 1998. Print.

Paul McHugh is a prominent professor of psychiatry at the Johns Hopkins School of Medicine. His name has become synonymous with the demystification of psychiatry. *The Perspectives of Psychiatry* is a landmark text he wrote with his department colleague Phillip R. Slavney, the Eugene Meyer III Professor Emeritus of Psychiatry and Medicine.

No research would be complete without consideration of the basic patterns and constituent elements of psychiatric reasoning. I have a much greater appreciation for the challenges they face as a result of my research in this area. McHugh and Slaveny advise: "Psychiatrists are physicians devoted to identifying and treating human mental disorders. The truth is that the teaching of psychiatry is anomalous. In contrast to internal medicine, surgery, or pediatrics, psychiatry does not—indeed, it cannot—emerge straightforwardly from the course of study in physics, chemistry, and biology that medical students have followed since college. This is an unavoidable effect of the brain-mind problem. While scientists know how and why the heart functions, they simply do not yet know how the brain generates the mind. In contrast to cardiologists, psychiatrists cannot go directly from knowing the elements of the brain (neurons and synapses) to explaining the conscious experiences that are the essence of mental life."

This book was highly recommended after a discussion with a leading pediatric neurosurgeon. It provides a basis in theory for some of the major conceptual themes of mind-bugs. The authors explain: "many would define the term *mind* as the conceptualized repository of the conscious experience encompassing a person's thoughts, moods, and perceptions. It also consists of specific psychological capacities such as memory, perception, and emotional responses. Finally, the mind is the "setting" of executive purpose, that is, it interprets the world and generates action. The brain, like a computer, can either have a broken part or take up maladaptive instructions and thus produce different mental conditions." These "maladaptive instructions" are what I am calling mind-bugs.

If you have stuck with me so far, you understand then that all psychiatry is based on modes of explanation. It is then unarguable that I also must rely on models like mind-bugs to address the observed features of decision disorders.

For those that want to delve further, this book represents the accumulated wisdom of two highly-regarded psychiatrists who were in the position of teaching Johns Hopkins medical students. It also promotes the relationship with groups that surround psychiatry such as psychology, anthropology, sociology, biological sciences, neurology, medicine, epidemiology, and the patient perspective. Per McHugh and Slaveny: "All progress in psychiatric investigation will depend on the facilitation of similar linkages between psychiatrists and other investigative workers."

A master of the pointed one-liner, McHugh introduced a series of them into the departmental repertoire over the years. First and foremost was: "What do we know and how do we know it?" It's a question designed to keep psychiatrists away from flights of theoretical fancy and teach residents to keep their feet on solid scientific ground. "Teaching psychiatry is often like practicing psychotherapy," McHugh says. "You have to drive ideas out of people's heads first, before you go on to fill them with others."

The book is written for psychiatrists and advanced students.

2. Cellular and Molecular Neurobiology

LeDoux, Joseph. *"The Emotional Brain, Fear, and the Amygdala."* Cellular and Molecular Neurobiology 23.4/5 (2003): 727-38. Print.

Joseph E. LeDoux, a neuroscientist, is the Henry and Lucy Moses Professor of Science, and Professor of Neuroscience and Psychology at New York University. He is also the director of the Center for the Neuroscience of Fear and Anxiety, a multi-university Center in New York City devoted to using animal research to understand pathological fear and anxiety in humans. LeDoux's research interests are mainly focused on the biological underpinnings of memory and emotion, especially the mechanisms of fear.

Ledoux advises: "In the late 1970s and early '80s, researchers began using a simple behavioral task, Pavlovian fear conditioning, to study fear networks. This made all the difference.

"In Pavlovian fear conditioning, an emotionally neutral conditioned stimulus (CS), usually a tone, is presented in conjunction with an aversive unconditioned stimulus (US), often foot shock. After one or several pairings, the CS acquires the capacity to elicit responses that typically occur in the presence of danger, such as defensive behavior (freezing or escape responses), autonomic nervous system responses (changes in blood pressure and heart rate), neuroendocrine responses (release of hormones from the pituitary and adrenal glands), etc. The responses are not learned and are not voluntary. They are innate, species-typical responses to threats and are expressed automatically in the presence of appropriate stimuli. Fear conditioning thus allows new or learned threats to automatically activate evolutionarily-tuned ways of responding to danger."

LeDoux goes on to advise that with key elements of the circuitry identified, researchers have turned to questions about the cellular and molecular basis of fear conditioning. He finds two amygdala pathways in the brain of the laboratory mouse by the use of fear conditioning and lesion study. He names them the "high road" and "low road". The low road is a pathway which is able to transmit a signal from a stimulus to the thalamus, and then to the amygdala, which then activates a fear-response in the body. This sequence works without a conscious experience of what comprises the stimulus, and it is the fast way to a bodily response. The high road is activated simultaneously. This is a slower road which also includes the cortical parts of the brain, thus creating a conscious impression of what the stimulus is. The low road only involves the sub-cortical part of the brain. It is therefore regarded as a more primitive mechanism of defense, only existing in its separate form in lesser-developed animals who have not developed the more complex part of the brain. In more developed animals the high road and the low road work simultaneously to provide both fear-response and perceptual feedback.

The way we respond to fear is a fundamental theme of mind-bugs. LeDoux's work provides a significant technical base for those interested in delving deeper.

3. Psychology

Gilovich, Thomas. *How We Know What Isn't So: the Fallibility of Human Reason in Everyday Life.* **New York: Free, 1993. Print.**

Thomas Gilovich is Professor and Chairperson in the Department of Psychology at Cornell University. He describes himself: "My research deals with how people evaluate the evidence of their everyday experience to make judgments, form beliefs, and decide on courses of action, and how they sometimes misevaluate that evidence and make faulty judgments, form dubious beliefs, and embark on counterproductive courses of action. I am also interested in the emotional states that both influence and follow from people's judgments." He has collaborated with the well-known researchers Daniel Kahneman, Lee Ross, and Amos Tversky and together they've researched and written on decision-making and behavioral economics.

Gilovich's exposé of the fallibility of human reasoning in everyday life advises that we all often tell ourselves lies; that if you want to believe it's true, it is; and that humans can't help seeing patterns where none exist. Failure to record negative outcomes, faulty reasoning from incomplete or ambiguous data, a tendency to seek out "hypothesis-confirming evidence", and the habit of self-serving belief are among the factors Gilovich pinpoints in his sophisticated analysis. And he discusses deeper motives, fear, prospects of power, and similar traits that fortify superstitions and the will to believe.

If you have read this book then you likely can relate the underlying research, discoveries, facts, and observations that Gilovich and many others have contributed to supporting many of the individual mind-bugs. I choose to provide simple to understand terminology and to use the metaphor of mind-bugs to improve the ease at which readers can relate and improve their decisions. But, my collection of mind-bugs was screened from a broad collection of mistakes of reason by many researchers like Gilovich.

Taylor, Jim. "Prime Business: More to Fear than Fear Itself." *Psychology Today.* Sussex Publishers, LLC, 27 July 2009. Web.

Dr. Taylor has a Ph.D. from the University of Colorado, Boulder, with a major field of Personality and Social Psychology and minor field of Clinical Psychology. In this article he presents an easy to understand summary of the "fight-or-flight response". My purpose of providing this is to point to the insights of the research rather than limit this section to only research.

The typical human reaction to crisis is best known as the "fight-or-flight" response that has evolved in humans over millions of years with a singular purpose: to ensure our survival. The primitive humans who had this reaction had a better chance of survival and passed on those genes to future generations up to the present. This crisis mentality has three components: fear, negativity, and panic. Fear prepared us physiologically to fight or flee by increasing our strength and stamina, sharpening our senses, and reducing our perception of pain. Focusing on the negative dimensions of the crisis, namely, the immediate threat, ensured that we stayed vigilant to the most apparent dangers, allowing us to respond most quickly. Panic created instantaneous action, either frenetic resistance or rapid flight, that made survival more likely. This reaction was very effective back in primitive times because the threats back then were generally immediate and simple.

Unfortunately, survival is much more complex today. As a result, the crisis psychology of primitive times simply won't work any longer. Fear paralyzes our ability to think clearly, solve problems, and make decisions. Negativity becomes a self-fulfilling prophecy. And panic causes knee-jerk and ill-advised reactions.

"Stress: The Fight or Flight Response." *Psychologist World.com.* Psychologist World. Web.

Here is another overview of the fight-or-flight response from *Psychologist World*, a curator of knowledge in the field of psychology. It references the originator of the fight-or-flight response and points further to the physiological reactions.

The flight-or-fight response, also called the "acute stress response" was first described by Walter Cannon in the 1920s as a theory that animals react to threats with a general discharge of the sympathetic nervous system. The response was later recognized as the first stage of a general adaptation syndrome that regulates stress responses among vertebrates and other organisms.

The onset of a stress response is associated with specific physiological actions in the sympathetic nervous system, primarily caused by release of chemicals into the body. These facilitate immediate physical reactions by triggering increases in heart rate and breathing, constricting blood vessels, and tightening muscles.

If a stimulus is perceived as a threat, a more intense and prolonged discharge of the locus ceruleus activates the sympathetic division of the autonomic nervous system (Thase & Howland, 1995). The activation of the sympathetic nervous system leads to the release of norepinephrine from nerve endings acting on the heart, blood vessels, respiratory centers, and other sites. The ensuing physiological changes constitute a major part of the acute stress response.

4. Neuroscience and Neuropsychology

Gazzaniga, Michael S. *Human: the Science behind What Makes Us Unique.* New York: Ecco, 2008. Print.

Michael S. Gazzaniga is the director of the University of California-Santa Barbara's SAGE Center for the Study of the Mind, as well as its Summer Institute in Cognitive Neuroscience. He is one of the world's leading neuroscientists and explores how best to understand the human condition by examining the biological, psychological, and highly social nature of our species. Per Steven Pinker, a well-respected professor, having been in both the Department of Psychology at Harvard and Department of Brain and Cognitive Science at MIT: "This is the place to look to learn about our best scientific understanding of what it means to be human."

To quote Gazzaniga: "To be sure, the human brain is a bizarre device, set in place through natural selection for one main purpose—to make decisions that enhance reproductive success and survival. It has approximately one hundred billion neurons, and each, on average, connects to about one thousand other neurons resulting in one hundred trillion synaptical connections. Even though it may not seem so, our consciousness is rather kicked back and relaxed when you think about all the input with which the brain is being bombarded and the processing that is going on. Only certain information makes it through to consciousness. Experiments have shown that in order for a stimulus to reach consciousness, it needs a minimal amount of time to be present, and it needs to have a certain degree of clarity. However, this is not quite enough. The stimulus has to have an interaction with the attention state of the observer. Attention and consciousness are two separate animals."

He further states: "The system that started out making sense of all the information bombarding the brain—interpreting our cognitive and emotional responses to what we encounter in our environment—also creates a running narrative of our actions, emotions, thoughts, and dreams. Belief formation comes in two flavors. Neuropsychologist Justin Barret calls these two systems reflective and non-reflective. Non-reflective beliefs are fast and automatic. It is as if we are not yet comfortable with our rational, analytical mind. In terms of evolution, it is a new ability that we humans have recently come upon, and we appear to use it sparingly.

When are we motivated to think rationally? Well, we are motivated when we want to find the optimal solution. But what is the optimal solution? Is it the actual truth, or is it one that verifies how you see the world, or one that maintains your status and reputation? We have to have enough time to think about it so the automatic response doesn't kick in. Research has shown that people will use the first argument that satisfies their opinion and then stop thinking."

As the author, I could continue; however, I hope the points of connection to our model have been at least sufficiently initiated.

5. Neurobiology

Panzer, A., M. Viljoen, and J. L. Roos. "The Neurobiological Basis of Fear: a Concise Review." *South African Psychiatry Review* May (2007): 71-75. Print.

The authors are respected researchers in the Departments of Physiology and Psychiatry at the School of Health Sciences, University of Pretoria, Pretoria, South Africa.

The fear pathways have been widely studied, initially through animal experiences and more recently through brain-imaging studies in humans. This short, well-referenced scientific article connects fear and anxiety with many shared neuro-anatomical and neuro-chemical characteristics. It reports that the fear reaction helped animals to survive a present danger, for example by freezing and thus not attracting a predator's attention. Other research has shown that it works the same in humans. Associated with the fear response is the release of a cascade of chemicals to mobilize resources in the short run and shut down unnecessary systems.

Feeling fear also helps to predict future threats. But if we learn to associate innocent stimuli with danger (as in perceived social threats) this same fear response is triggered. Fear conditioning is the ability of an innocent trigger to unleash the reaction, particularly conditioning that occurs below conscious level where impulses are transmitted via direct pathway from the thalamus to the amygdala. When fear persists although there is no danger, precious physical and mental resources are squandered.

The fear response travels on a direct pathway by way of the amygdala, leading to rapid reaction to relatively simple unprocessed perceptual information. The indirect pathway takes longer and delivers information analyzed in terms of various modalities like rational thinking. So when our reactions are fear-based, rational thinking takes a back seat.

6. Social Cognitive Neuroscience

Social cognitive neuroscience (SCN) is an interdisciplinary field that asks questions about topics traditionally of interest to social psychologists (such as emotion regulation, attitude change, or stereotyping) using methods traditionally employed by cognitive neuroscientists (such as functional brain imaging and neuropsychological patient analysis). Here are three papers that provide a connection between social pain and the parts of the brain that are involved with the fear reaction.

Eisenberger, N. I. "Does Rejection Hurt? An FMRI Study of Social Exclusion." *Science* 302.5643 (2003): 290-92. Print

- Naomi Eisenberger is director of the Social and Affective Neuroscience laboratory as well as co-director of the Social Cognitive Neuroscience Laboratory at UCLA.
- Matthew D Lieberman, PhD, is Professor, SCN Lab Co-Director. He is UCLA associate professor of psychology and a founder of social cognitive neuroscience.
- Kipling D. Williams is a social psychologist in the Department of Psychological Science at Purdue University in West Lafayette, Indiana. Dr. Williams has conducted research in several areas, including aggression, group processes, and close relationships.

This article overviews the authors' neuro-imaging study that examined the neural correlates of social exclusion and tested the hypothesis that the brain bases of social pain are similar to those of physical pain. Participants were scanned while playing a virtual ball-tossing game in which they were ultimately excluded.

As it relates to mind-bugs the study reports: "It is a basic feature of human experience to feel soothed in the presence of others and to feel distressed when left behind". Evidence suggests that some of the same neural machinery recruited in the experience of physical pain may also be involved in the experience of pain associated with social separation or rejection.

The authors conducted a functional magnetic resonance imaging (fMRI) study of social exclusion to determine whether the regions activated by social pain are similar to those found in studies of physical pain. Given that even the mildest forms of social exclusion can generate social pain, the authors investigated the neural response during two types of social exclusion: (i) explicit social exclusion (ESE), in which individuals were prevented from participating in a social activity by other players engaged in the social activity, and (ii) implicit social exclusion (ISE), in which participants, because of extenuating circumstances, were not able to join in a social activity with other players.

In summary, a pattern of activations very similar to those found in studies of physical pain emerged during social exclusion, providing evidence that the experience and regulation of social and physical pain share a common neuro-anatomical basis. This study suggests that social pain is analogous in its neuro-cognitive function to physical pain, alerting us when we have sustained injury to our social connections, allowing restorative measures to be taken. Understanding the underlying commonalities between physical and social pain unearths new perspectives on issues such as why physical and social pain are affected similarly by both social support and neuro-chemical interventions, and why it "hurts" to lose someone we love (and likely something we desire).

Lieberman, M. D., and N. I. Eisenberger. "NEUROSCIENCE: Pains and Pleasures of Social Life." *Science* 323.5916 (2009): 890-91. Print.

(Authors previously introduced)

This article states: "Life is full of complex social events such as being accepted or rejected, treated fairly or unfairly, and esteemed or devalued by others. Our responses to these events depend primarily on our psychological interpretation of them, in contrast to events like spraining an ankle or eating chocolate, for which our responses seem more dependent on the physical acts themselves. Nevertheless, our emotional responses to these psychological events rely on much of the same neural circuitry that underlies the simplest physical pains and pleasures. ...

"Although it is expected that these [brain] networks produce robust responses to physical pains and pleasures, it is surprising that social pains and pleasures activate these same networks. For example, being socially excluded activates the dACC and insula, with the dACC showing greater activity to the extent that an individual feels greater social pain. Grieving over the death of a loved one and being treated unfairly also activate these regions. Alternatively, social rewards activate the same reward network as desirable foods and drinks. Having a good reputation, being treated fairly, and being cooperative all activate the ventral striatum. Strikingly, making charitable donations activates the reward network more than receiving the same sum of money for oneself. ...

"Takahashi *et al.* demonstrate, for the first time, this dynamic interplay between social pains and pleasures. If maintaining one's social value is a need like other physical needs, then the greater the pain caused by negative social comparisons, the greater the pleasure in response to seeing the comparison target socially devalued (schadenfreude). The authors found that greater envy and dACC activity in response to a negative social comparison was associated with greater schadenfreude and ventral striatum activity when learning of that comparison target's subsequent downfall."

"In addition to the caregiver-infant bond, connections to a social group also promote survival. When responsibility for food acquisition, protection from predators, and care for offspring are distributed among group members (rather than being the sole responsibility of a single individual), individual group members are more likely to survive. Being fair, cooperative, or charitable may increase the survival of the group and thus one's own offspring. Moreover, group members who are not cooperative are more likely to be ostracized, which greatly lowers chances of survival. Thus, evolutionary pressures may have created internal mechanisms that register being socially cooperative as pleasurable and being ostracized as painful in order to promote the maintenance of group bonds and ensure survival.

"The link between social and physical pains and pleasures adds to the growing chorus of neuro-cognitive findings that point to the critical importance of the social world for the surviving and thriving of humans. Our attentiveness to the social world may sometimes seem like a diversion from more concrete concerns, but increasingly, neuroscience is revealing ways in which such attention is actually an adaptive response to some of our most vital concerns."

"Human Brain Appears 'Hard-wired' for Hierarchy." PhysOrg. com - Science News, Technology, Physics, Nanotechnology, Space Science, Earth Science, Medicine. Web. 22 Dec. 2010

Human imaging studies have for the first time identified brain circuitry associated with social status, according to researchers at the National Institute of Mental Health (NIMH) of the National Institutes of Health. They found that different brain areas are activated when a person moves up or down in a pecking order—or simply views perceived social superiors or inferiors. Circuitry activated by important events responded to a potential change in hierarchical status as much as it did to winning money.

"Our position in social hierarchies strongly influences motivation as well as physical and mental health," said NIMH Director Thomas R Insel, M.D. "This first glimpse into how the brain processes that information advances our understanding of an important factor that can impact public health."

7. NeuroLeadership

Thanks to my close friend David Baumgarten, who is working on his Masters in NeuroLeadership, I was introduced to and joined the NeuroLeadership Institute. NeuroLeadership is an emerging field of study focused on bringing neuro-scientific knowledge into the areas of leadership development, management training, change management, education, consulting, and coaching. These articles are but a few that are available and well-grounded in research.

Rock, David. "SCARF: a Brain-based Model for Collaborating with and Influencing Others." *NeuroLeadership Journal* **One (2008).** *www.NeuroLeadership.org.* **NeuroLeadership Institute, 2008. Web. 2009.**

In late 2006, David Rock founded the NeuroLeadership Institute and Summit, a global initiative bringing neuroscientists and leadership experts together to build a new science of leadership development. The Institute is now a worldwide network of researchers and practitioners building a new body of knowledge. David is on the advisory board at CIMBA business school, and a guest lecturer at universities in five countries including Oxford University Said Business School.

In his SCARF model Rock proposes how threats and rewards might be managed in five domains: status, certainty, autonomy, relatedness, and fairness. It is based on some of the research highlighted elsewhere in this section, in the references, and as included in Rock's article.

Lieberman, Mathew. "The Brain's Braking System (and How to 'Use Your Words' to Tap into It.)." *NeuroLeadership Journal* Issue Two (2009): 9-14. Print.

(Author previously introduced)

This review examines work that together suggests that RVLPFC is a central part of the brain's braking system, supporting self-control in its various forms. Neuroscience makes an important contribution here because the different forms of self-control feel so different from one another it would be easy to assume that the underlying processes supporting self-control in each case have little in common. "We have also demonstrated evidence suggesting that putting feelings into words serves as an unexpected gateway into the brain's braking system, setting self-control processes in motion without the individual intentionally trying to engage in self-control. Lastly, we have found some promising evidence that people can strengthen the impact of putting feelings into words through mindful meditative practice. Of course, we may just be scratching the surface. The fact that mindfulness training may produce benefits in no way means that this is the only route or the best route towards improving the functioning of this process. Nevertheless, it's important to find out that this process is malleable, allowing for future investigations to examine other ways in which the brain's braking system can be made to work to our benefit."

McDonald, Paul. "The Potential Contribution of Neuroscience to Authentic Leadership." *NeuroLeadership Journal* Issue Two (2009): 53-66. Print

McDonald is Senior Lecturer, Victoria Management School, Victoria University of Wellington.

This article is focused on the contribution of neuroscience to four factors of authentic leadership: self-awareness, relational transparency, balanced processing, and internalized moral perspective. Under each factor, a number of research intersections have been recognized with both theoretical and developmental implications. It is important to recognize that authentic leadership research (Walumbwa, et aI., 2008) devotes considerable attention to additional constructs such as organizational culture, climate, and the nature of relations between authentic Neurological Correlates to Authentic Leadership leaders and their followers.

For example, neuroscience research on mirror neurons (Gazzaniga, 2004) has the potential to inform the development of authentic followers. Mirror neurons exist throughout the brain. The interesting point is that they fire, not only when we behave, but also when we observe the behavior of others. Watching an action creates the same neural signatures as doing the actions themselves. Therefore, the challenge to authentic leaders is to develop followers in a manner that utilizes our knowledge of mirror neurons, including: acting as a mentor, being visible as a role model and coach, and using salient visual (as well as auditory and word) data to communicate expectations (Goleman & Boyatzis, 2008).

8. Behavioral Economics

Ariely, Dan. Predictably Irrational: the Hidden Forces That Shape Our Decisions. New York, NY: Harper, 2009. Print.

Ariely taught at MIT before returning to Duke University as James B. Duke Professor of Psychology and Behavioral Economics. He has spent over 20 years researching these topics. In this bestselling book he provides the following insights to what I group and categorize as mind-bugs:

"Irrational behavior is a part of human nature. People tend to behave irrationally in a predictable fashion. Drawing on psychology and economics, behavioral economics can show us why cautious people make poor decisions about sex when aroused, why patients get greater relief from a more expensive drug over its cheaper counterpart, and why honest people may steal office supplies or communal food, but not money."

According to Ariely, our understanding of economics, now based on the assumption of a rational subject, should, in fact, be based on our systematic, unsurprising irrationality. Ariely argues that greater understanding of previously ignored or misunderstood forces (emotions, relativity, and social norms) that influence our economic behavior brings a variety of opportunities for re-examining individual motivation and consumer choice, as well as economic and educational policy.

9. Cosmology and Physics

Hawking, S. W., and Leonard Mlodinow. *The Grand Design*. New York: Bantam, 2010. Print.

Why include cosmology and physics? It is an example of the breadth of scientific fields and well-respected individuals that are pointing to the underlying themes of mind-bugs. The celebrated University of Cambridge cosmologist Hawking, along with Caltech physicist Mlodinow, deftly mix cutting-edge physics in this bestselling book to answer key questions. They advise:

"Recent experiments in neuroscience support the view that it is our physical brain, following the known laws of science that determines our actions, and not some agency that exists outside those laws. For example, a study of patients undergoing awake brain surgery found that by electrically stimulating the appropriate regions of the brain, one could create in the patient the desire to move the hand, arm, or foot, or to move the lips and talk. It is hard to imagine how free will can operate if our behavior is determined by physical law, so it seems that we are no more than biological machines and that free will is just an illusion. In the case of people, since we cannot solve the equations that determine our behavior, we use the effective theory that people have free will. The study of our will, and of the behavior that arises from it, is the science of psychology. Economics is also an effective theory, based on the notion of free will plus the assumption that people evaluate their possible alternative courses of action and choose the best. That effective theory is only moderately successful in predicting behavior because, as we all know, decisions are often not rational or are based on a defective analysis of the consequences of the choice. That is why the world is in such a mess."

10. Critical Thinking

Paul, Richard, and Linda Elder. *Critical Thinking: Tools for Taking Charge of Your Professional and Personal Life*. Upper Saddle River, NJ: Financial Times/Prentice Hall, 2002. Print.

Richard Paul is Director of Research and Professional Development at the Center for Critical Thinking and Chair of the National Council for Excellence in Critical Thinking. Dr. Paul is an internationally recognized authority on critical thinking, with eight books and over 200 articles on the subject.

Dr. Linda Elder is an educational psychologist and a prominent authority on critical thinking. She is President of the Foundation for Critical Thinking and Executive Director of the Center for Critical Thinking. Dr. Elder has taught psychology and critical thinking at the college level and has given presentations to more than 20,000 educators at all levels.

In this book, the well-regarded Paul and Elder say: "You are what you think. Everything you do in life is determined by the quality of your thinking. If you aren't thinking clearly, you're at the mercy of everyone else—from dishonest politicians to aggressive, stop-at-nothing ad agencies. Unfortunately, many people never give any thought to how they think. No wonder they're susceptible to the frustration, pain, ineffectiveness, and financial loss that result directly from poorly-considered thinking. Critical Thinking is about becoming a better thinker in every aspect of your life—as a professional, as a consumer, citizen, friend, parent, and even as a lover."

They describe first-order thinking as spontaneous and non-reflective, containing both good and bad reasoning. Second-order thinking is where we consciously analyze and assess our thinking. The concept of mind-bugs is built on these same underlying aspects of human nature. While much research exists, Paul and Elder present the facts with emphasis on grounding them in the standards, elements, and intellectual traits of critical thinking.

11. Spirituality and Psychology

Easwaran, Eknath. *Conquest of Mind*. Tomales, CA: Nilgiri, 2001. Print.

Eknath Easwaran is respected as an authentic guide to timeless wisdom. He was a professor of English literature in India before coming to the United States in 1959 on the Fulbright exchange program. In 1961 he founded the Blue Mountain Center of Meditation which carries on his work today through publications and retreats.

This is a wonderful read for the spiritually-minded with a psychological bent. Eknath Easwaran writes: "Nothing can be more important than being able to choose the way we think—our feelings, aspirations, and desires; the way we view our world and ourselves. When we have a strong liking or disliking for something, we cannot really see that thing for what it is. A fog comes between us and that object, a fog of potential obsession. Our attention is not really on the thing in question; it is locked onto our liking or disliking. The mind is very much like a television set with no controls, which goes on when the mood strikes it and shows whatever it pleases. One of the major difficulties in learning to train the mind is that it is so hard to stand back and see our thoughts clearly. The mind—everybody's mind—is a vast factory, producing a continuous stream of thoughts of every description. If our thinking is based on stimulus and response, then most of us live like puppets, moved by patterns of thinking built up over years of repetition. These habits of mind cause us to say and do certain things habitually. They motivate our actions and mouth our words, and we just go along."

Tolle, Eckhart. *A New Earth: Awakening to Your Life's Purpose.* New York: Plume, 2006. Print.

Eckhart Tolle is a German-born writer, public speaker, and spiritual teacher. He is the author of the bestsellers, *The Power of Now* and *A New Earth.*

Tolle has sold millions of books with a basic message: "the most significant thing that can happen to a human being is the separation process of thinking and awareness." Whatever behavior unobserved thinking manifests, the hidden motivating force is always the same: the need to stand out, be special, be in control; the need for power, for attention, for more. Adding to those is the need to feel a sense of separation, that is to say, the need for opposition, the need for enemies. The underlying emotion that governs all the activity is fear. All that is required to become free of it is awareness.

The Science of Mindfulness

Dr. Ellen Langer is a professor in the Psychology Department at Harvard University. Dr. Langer is a Fellow of The Sloan Foundation; The American Psychological Association, the American Psychological Society, The American Association for the Advancement of Science, Computers and Society; The Society for the Psychological Study of Social Issues; The Society of Experimental Social Psychologists. Her books written for general and academic readers include *Mindfulness* and *The Power of Mindful Learning,* and the forthcoming *Mindful Creativity.*

Dr. Langer has described her work on the illusion of control, aging, decision-making, and mindfulness theory in over 200 research articles and six academic books. Her work has led to numerous academic honors including a Guggenheim Fellowship, the Award for Distinguished Contributions to Psychology in the Public Interest of the American Psychological Association, the Distinguished Contributions of Basic Science to Applied Psychology award from the American Association of Applied & Preventive Psychology, the James McKeen Cattel Award, and the Gordon Allport Intergroup Relations Prize.

Here are a few quotes from Dr. Langer's work: "Unlike the exotic altered states of consciousness that we read so much about, mindfulness and mindlessness are so common that few of us appreciate their importance or make use of their power to change our lives." "Mindlessness sets in when we rely too rigidly on categories and distinctions created in the past." "Another way that we become mindless is by forming a mindset when we first encounter something and then clinging to it when we re-encounter that same thing." "Because such mindsets form before we do much reflection, we call them premature cognitive commitments." "We are all frequently in error, but rarely in doubt."

So There You Have It

The underlying themes of the mind-bug model have been laid out and correlated with research abstracts. I hope you enjoyed this shallow dive and that you get a sense of the structures underneath mind-bugs. For those who want to go deeper, additional references are provided in Appendix D. I welcome and encourage challenge to my theories and approaches as part of continuous improvement and personal growth. It is only when we free ourselves of the effect of mind-bugs that our decisions and actions can be liberated from our own bias.

Appendix D: References

1. Alain Morin, Levels of Consciousness and Self-awareness: A Comparison and Integration of Various Views | PhilPapers." *PhilPapers: Online Research in Philosophy.* Web.
2. Anderson, Barry F. *The Three Secrets of Wise Decision Making.* Portland, OR: Single Reef, 2002. Print.
3. Argyris, Chris. *Flawed Advice and the Management Trap: How Managers Can Know When They're Getting Good Advice and When They're Not.* Oxford: Oxford UP, 2009. Print.
4. Argyris, Chris. *Reasons and Rationalizations the Limits to Organizational Knowledge.* Oxford: Oxford UP, 2006. Print.
5. Ariely, Dan, and Olivier Sibony. "Dan Ariely on Irrationality in the Workplace." *McKinsey Quarterly* (2011). Print.
6. Ariely, Dan. *Predictably Irrational: the Hidden Forces That Shape Our Decisions.* New York, NY: Harper, 2009. Print.
7. Arnsten, Amy F.T. "The Biology of Being Frazzled." *Science* 280.5370 (1998): 1711-712. Print.

8. Assaraf, John, and Murray Smith. *The Answer: Grow Any Business, Achieve Financial Freedom, and Live an Extraordinary Life.* New York: Atria, 2008. Print.

9. Baddeley, Alan D. *Working Memory.* Oxford [Oxfordshire: Clarendon, 1986. Print.

10. Barrett, Lisa Feldman. "A New Model for Emotion & Cognition." NeuroLeadership Summit. Boston USA. 26 Oct. 2010. Lecture.

11. Bandyopadhyay, Sourav, Et Al. "Rewiring of Genetic Networks in Response to DNA Damage." *Dec. 2, 2010, Issue of the Journal Science* Vol. 330.6009 (2010): 1385-389. Print.

12. Bargh, John A. "Attention and Automaticity in the Processing of Self-relevant Information." *Journal of Personality and Social Psychology* 43.3 (1982): 425-36. Print.

13. Bargh, John A., Mark Chen, and Lara Burrows. "Automaticity of Social Behavior: Direct Effects of Trait Construct and Stereotype Activation on Action." *Journal of Personality and Social Psychology* 71.2 (1996): 230-44. Print.

14. Barrett, Lisa Feldman, Batja Mesquita, Kevin N. Ochsner, and James J. Gross. "The Experience of Emotion." *Annual Review of Psychology* 58.1 (2007): 373-403. Print.

15. "The Basic Laws of Human Stupidity." *Fravia R.I.P.* Web. <http://www.searchlores.org/realicra/basiclawsofhumanstupidity.htm>.

16. Baumgarten, David. "How Neuroscientists Seem to Be Using Words and Definitions." E-mail interview. 4 Jan. 2011.

17. Begley, Sharon. "Can You Build a Better Brain?" *Newsweek* 10 Jan. 2011: 40-45. Print.

18. Begley, Sharon. "I Can't Think." *Newsweek* 7 Mar. 2011. Print.

19. Begley, Sharon. "The Limits of Reason." *Newsweek* 16 Aug. 2010: 24. Print.

20. Begley, Sharon. *Train Your Mind, Change Your Brain: How a New Science Reveals Our Extraordinary Potential to Transform Ourselves.* New York: Ballantine, 2008. Print.

21. Bem, Daryl J. "The Self-perception Theory." *Advances in Experimental Social Psychology* 6 (1972). Print.

22. Bodner, T., and E. Langer. *Individual Differences in Mindfulness: The Langer Mindfulness Scale. Poster Session Presented at the Annual Meeting of the American Psychological Society, Toronto, Ont., Canada.* 2001. Print.

23. Bodner, T., and E. Langer. "Toronto, Ont., Canada." *Individual Differences in Mindfulness: The Langer Mindfulness Scale.* Proc. of Annual Meeting of The American Psychological Society, Poster Session, Toronto, Canada. 2001. Print.

24. Brafman, Ori, and Rom Brafman. *Sway: the Irresistible Pull of Irrational Behavior.* New York: Doubleday, 2008. Print.

25. Braza, Jerry. *Moment by Moment: the Art and Practice of Mindfulness.* Boston: C.E. Tuttle, 1997. Print.

26. Brothers, Leslie. *Friday's Footprint: How Society Shapes the Human Mind.* New York: Oxford UP, 1997. Print.

27. Brown, K. W., and R. M. Ryan. "The Benefits of Being Present: Mindfulness and Its Role in Psychological Well Being." *Journal of Personality and Social Psychology* 84 (2003): 822-48. Print.

28. Brown, Kirk Warren, and Richard M. Ryan. "Perils and Promise in Defining and Measuring Mindfulness: Observations From Experience." *Clinical Psychology: Science and Practice* September 11.3 (2004): 242-48. Print.

29. Brown, Paul, Tara Swart, and Jane Meyler. "Emotional Intelligence." *Neuro-Leadership Journal* Issue Two (2009): 67-77. Print.

30. Campbell, Andrew, and Jo Whitehead. "How to Test Your Decision Making Instincts." *McKinsey Quarterly* (May 2010). Print.

31. Cannon, Walter B. *The Wisdom of the Body.* New York: W.W. Norton &, 1939. Print.

32. Carroll, Robert Todd. *Becoming a Critical Thinker: a Guide for the New Millennium.* Needham Heights, MA: Pearson Custom Pub., 2000. Print.

33. Charney, D. S., C. Grillon, and J. D. Bremner. "Review: The Neurobiological Basis of Anxiety and Fear: Circuits, Mechanisms, and Neurochemical Interactions (Part I." *The Neuroscientist* 4.1 (1998): 35-44. Print.

34. Cialdini, Robert B. *Influence: the Psychology of Persuasion.* New York: Collins, 2007. Print.

35. Cooper, David A. *God Is a Verb: Kabbalah and the Practice of Mystical Judaism.* New York: Riverhead, 1997. Print.

36. Custers, Ruud, and Henk Aarts. "The Unconscious Will: How the Pursuit of Goals Operates Outside of Conscious Awareness." *Science.* American Association for the Advancement of Science, 1 July 2010. Web.

37. Davidson Et Al, Alterations in Brain and Immune Function Produced by Mindfulness Meditation 65 (4): 564." *Psychosomatic Medicine.* 2003. Web. <http://www.psychosomaticmedicine.org/content/65/4/564.full.pdf>.

38. "Debugging Basics: Breakpoints." *MSDN | Microsoft Development, Subscriptions, Resources, and More.* Microsoft. Web. 09 Jan. 2011. <http://msdn.microsoft.com/en-us/library/4607yxb0(v=vs.80).aspx>.

39. "Discovery Health "How Fear Works"" *Discovery Health "Health Guides"* Web. 08 Sept. 2010.

40. Easwaran, Eknath. *Conquest of Mind.* Tomales, CA: Nilgiri, 2001. Print.

41. Easwaran, Eknath. *The Bhagavad Gita.* Tomales, CA: Nilgiri, 2007. Print.

42. Easwaran, Eknath. *Words to Live By: a Daily Guide to Leading an Exceptional Life.* Tomales, CA: Nilgiri, 2005. Print.

43. Eisenberger, N. I. "Does Rejection Hurt? An FMRI Study of Social Exclusion." *Science* 302.5643 (2003): 290-92. Print.

44. Faber, David. *And Then the Roof Caved In: How Wall Street's Greed and Stupidity Brought Capitalism to Its Knees.* Hoboken, NJ: John Wiley & Sons, 2009. Print.

45. Fauconnier, Gilles, and Mark Turner. *The Way We Think: Conceptual Blending and the Mind's Hidden Complexities.* New York: Basic, 2002. Print.

46. Feeney, Aidan, and Evan Heit. *Inductive Reasoning: Experimental, Developmental, and Computational Approaches.* Cambridge: Cambridge UP, 2007. Print.

47. Finkelstein, Sydney, Jo Whitehead, and Andrew Campbell. *Think Again: Why Good Leaders Make Bad Decisions and How to Keep It from Happening to You.* Boston, MA: Harvard Business, 2008. Print.

48. Folkes, Valerie S. "Mindlessness or Mindfulness: A Partial Replication and Extension of Langer, Blank, and Chanowitz." *Journal of Personality and Social Psychology* 48.3 (1985): 600-04. Print.

49. Follett, Mary Parker., Henry C. Metcalf, and L. Urwick. *Dynamic Administration: The Collected Papers of Mary Parker Follett.* London: Taylor & Francis, 2003. Print.

50. Gazzaniga, Michael S. *Human: the Science behind What Makes Us Unique.* New York: Ecco, 2008. Print.

51. Gilovich, Thomas. *How We Know What Isn't So: the Fallibility of Human Reason in Everyday Life.* New York: Free, 1993. Print.

52. Gladwell, Malcolm. *Blink: the Power of Thinking without Thinking.* New York: Little, Brown and, 2005. Print.

53. Goleman, Daniel. *Emotional Intelligence.* New York: Bantam, 2006. Print.

54. Goleman, Daniel, Richard E. Boyatzis, and Annie McKee. *Primal Leadership: Realizing the Power of Emotional Intelligence.* Boston, MA: Harvard Business School, 2002. Print.

55. Green, Thad B. *Motivation Management: Fueling Performance by Discovering What People Believe about Themselves and Their Organizations.* Palo Alto, CA: Davies-Black Pub., 2000. Print.

56. Hart, Leslie A. *Human Brain and Human Learning.* New York: Longman, 1983. Print.

57. *Harvard Business Review on Decision Making.* Boston: Harvard Business School, 2001. Print.

58. Haskins, Greg R. "A Practical Guide To Critical Thinking." *The Skeptic's Dictionary.* Web. 29 Apr. 2009.

59. Hawking, S. W., and Leonard Mlodinow. *The Grand Design.* New York: Bantam, 2010. Print.

60. Hawkins, David R. *Power vs. Force: the Hidden Determinants of Human Behavior.* Carlsbad, CA: Hay House, 2002. Print.

61. Hawkins, David R. *The Eye of the I.* W. Sedona, AZ: Veritas, 2002. Print.

62. Hawkins, David R. *Transcending the Levels of Consciousness.* Sedona, AZ: Veritas Pub., 2006. Print.

63. Hay Group. "Re-engaging with Engagement." *Business Research.* 2010. Web.

64. Herrnstein, Richard J., and Charles A. Murray. *The Bell Curve: Intelligence and Class Structure in American Life.* New York: Simon & Schuster, 1996. Print.

65. "Hidden Flaws in Strategy - McKinsey Quarterly - Strategy - Strategic Thinking." *Articles by McKinsey Quarterly: Online Business Journal of McKinsey & Company. Business Management Strategy - Corporate Strategy - Global Business Strategy.* Web. 10 Dec. 2010. <http://www.mckinseyquarterly.com/Hidden_flaws_in_strategy_1288>.

66. Hoch, Stephen James, Howard C. Kunreuther, and Robert E. Gunther. *Wharton on Making Decisions.* New York: John Wiley & Sons, 2001. Print.

67. Honderich, Ted. *The Oxford Companion to Philosophy.* Oxford: Oxford UP, 1995. Print.

68. "Human Brain Appears 'hard-wired' for Hierarchy." *PhysOrg.com - Science News, Technology, Physics, Nanotechnology, Space Science, Earth Science, Medicine.* Web. 22 Dec. 2010. <http://www.physorg.com/news128173846.html>.

69. "Infinite Loop." *Wikipedia, the Free Encyclopedia.* 2 May 2011. Web. <http://en.wikipedia.org/wiki/Infinite_loop>.

70. ING. *An Advisor's Guide to Behaviorial Finance.* New York: ING, 2008. Print.

71. Jacobs, Charles S. *Management Rewired: Why Feedback Doesn't Work and Other Surprising Lessons from the Latest Brain Science.* New York, NY: Portfolio, 2009. Print.

72. Janis, Irving L., and Leon Mann. *Decision Making: a Psychological Analysis of Conflict, Choice, and Commitment.* New York: Free, 1977. Print.

73. Janis, Irving L. *Groupthink: Psychological Studies of Policy Decisions and Fiascoes.* Boston: Houghton Mifflin, 1982. Print.

74. Jensen, Eric. *Brain-based Learning: the New Paradigm of Teaching.* Thousand Oaks, CA.: Corwin, 2008. Print.

75. Jensen, Eric. *Enriching the Brain: How to Maximize Every Learner's Potential.* San Francisco: Jossey-Bass, 2006. Print.

76. Kabat-Zinn, John. "Mindfulness-based Interventions in Context: Past, Present, and Future." *Clinical Psychology: Science and Practice* 10 (2003): 144-56. Print.

77. Kabat-Zinn, Jon. *Arriving at Your Own Door: 108 Lessons in Mindfulness.* New York: Hyperion, 2007. Print.

78. Kabat-Zinn, Jon. *Wherever You Go, There You Are: Mindfulness Meditation in Everyday Life.* New York: Hyperion, 1994. Print.

79. Kahneman, Daniel, and Gary Klein. "Conditions for Intuitive Expertise: A Failure to Disagree." *American Psychologist* 64.6 (2009): 515-26. Print.

80. Kahneman, Daniel, Paul Slovic, and Amos Tversky. *Judgment under Uncertainty: Heuristics and Biases.* Cambridge: Cambridge UP, 1982. Print.

81. Kanellos, Michael. "Video: Microsoft Attempts to Predict the Future | Epicenter | Wired.com." *Wired.com.* Conde Nast Digital, 10 May 2010. Web.

82. Kelsang, Gyatso. *How to Solve Our Human Problems: the Four Noble Truths.* Ulverston, England: Tharpa Publications, 2005. Print.

83. Kennedy, Alan, and Alan Wilkes. *Studies in Long Term Memory.* London: Wiley, 1975. Print. :3-18 Broadbent, D.E. (1975), The Magic Number Seven after Fifteen Years.

84. Kim, Jaegwon. "Thought." *Wikipedia, the Free Encyclopedia.* Web. 10 Jan. 2011. <http://en.wikipedia.org/wiki/Thought>.

85. Klein, Gary. "Performing a Project Premortem - Harvard Business Review." *Harvard Business Review Case Studies, Articles, Books.* Harvard Business Publishing, Sept. 2007. Web.

86. Kleiner, Art. "The Thought Leader Interview: Manfred F.R. Kets De Vries." *Strategy+Business* 59 (Summer 2010). Print.

87. Kleiner, By Art. "The Thought Leader Interview: Manfred F.R. Kets De Vries." *Strategy Business: International Business Strategy News Articles and Award-winning Analysis.* 10 May 2010. Web. <http://www.strategy-business.com/article/10209?gko=cbe31>.

88. Langer, Ellen J., and Robert P. Abelson. *The Psychology of Control.* Beverly Hills: Sage Publications, 1983. Print.

89. Langer, Ellen. "Mindful Leadership." NeuroLeadership Summit. Boston USA. 26 Oct. 2010. Lecture.

90. Langer, Ellen J. *Mindfulness.* Reading, MA: Addison-Wesley Pub., 1989. Print.

91. *Leadership and Self-deception: Getting out of the Box.* San Francisco, CA: Berrett-Koehler, 2002. Print.

92. LeDoux, Hoseph. "The Emotional Brain, Fear, and the Amygdala." *Cellular and Molecular Neurobiology* 23.4/5 (2003): 727-38. Print.

93. Lehrer, Jonah. *How We Decide.* Boston: Houghton Mifflin Harcourt, 2009. Print.

94. Lewis, Michael, Jeannette M. Haviland-Jones, and Lisa Feldman. Barrett. *Handbook of Emotions.* New York: Guilford, 2008. Print.

95. Lewis, Michael. *Panic: the Story of Modern Financial Insanity.* New York: W.W. Norton &, 2009. Print.

96. Lieberman, M. D., and N. I. Eisenberger. "NEUROSCIENCE: Pains and Pleasures of Social Life." *Science* 323.5916 (2009): 890-91. Print.

97. Lieberman, M., R. Gaunt, D. Gilbert, and Y. Trope. "Reflexion and Reflection: A Social Cognitive Neuroscience Approach to Attributional Inference." *Advances in Experimental Social Psychology* 34 (2002): 199-249. Print.

98. Lieberman, Mathew. "The Brain's Braking System (and How to 'use Your Words' to Tap into It.)." *NeuroLeadership Journal* Issue Two (2009): 9-14. Print.

99. Livraghi, Giancarlo. *The Power of Stupidity*. Pescara – Italy: Monti & Ambrosini. Print. May 2009.

100. Lovallo, Dan, and Olivier Sibony. "A Language to Discuss Biases." *Articles by McKinsey Quarterly: Online Business Journal of McKinsey & Company. Business Management Strategy - Corporate Strategy - Global Business Strategy*. McKinsey & Company, Apr. 2010. Web.

101. Lovallo, Dan, and Olivier Sibony. "Distortions and Deceptions in Strategic Decisions." *The Online Journal of McKinsey and Company* Feb (2006). Print.

102. Lovallo, Dan, and Olivier Sibony. "The Case for Behaviorial Strategy." *McKinsey Quarterly* (March 2010). Print.

103. Love, Angela, and Julie Maloney. "Mindfullness as Capacity: at the Threshold of Leadership's next Wave?" *NeuroLeadership Journal* Issue Two (2009): 94-100. Print.

104. Marmot, M. G. *The Status Syndrome: How Social Standing Affects Our Health and Longevity*. New York: Times, 2004. Print.

105. Marquardt, Michael J. *Leading with Questions: How Leaders Find the Right Solutions by Knowing What to Ask*. San Francisco: Jossey-Bass, 2005. Print.

106. Marston, William Moulton, C. Daly King, and Elizabeth Holloway Marston. *Integrative Psychology; a Study of Unit Response,*. London: K. Paul, Trench, Trubner, 1931. Print.

107. Marston, William Moulton. *Emotions of Normal People,*. London: K. Paul, Trench, Trubner &, 1928. Print.

108. Martin, Michael. "Understanding Fight or Flight." *Concealed Carry Fundamentals*. First ed. Vol. June 2010. Woodbury MN: Key House, 2010. 124-49. Print.

109. Mauss, I., C. Cook, J. Cheng, and J. Gross. "Individual Differences in Cognitive Reappraisal: Experiential and Physiological Responses to an Anger Provocation." *International Journal of Psychophysiology* 66.2 (2007): 116-24. Print.

110. Mayo Clinic Staff. "Beyond Shyness: Overcoming the Fear of Social Situations." *Mayo Clinic*. Mayo Foundation for Medical Education and Research,

27 Aug. 2003. Web. <http://www.nldline.com/overcoming_social_fears_mayo.htm>.

111. McDonald, Paul. "The Potential Contribution of Neuroscience to Authentic Leadership." *NeuroLeadership Journal* Issue Two (2009): 53-66. Print.

112. McHugh, Paul R., and Phillip R. Slavney. *The Perspectives of Psychiatry.* Baltimore: Johns Hopkins UP, 1998. Print.

113. Menkes, Justin. *Executive Intelligence: What All Great Leaders Have.* New York: Collins, 2005. Print.

114. Mitchell, Deborah J., J. Edward Russo, and Nancy Pennington. "Back to the Future: Temporal Perspective in the Explanation of Events." *Journal of Behaviorial Decision Making* 2 (1989): 25-38. Print.

115. Nelson, Randy Joe. *Biology of Aggression.* Oxford: Oxford UP, 2006. Print.

116. *NeuroLeadership Institute.* Web. 08 Sept. 2010. <http://www.neuroleadership.org/>.

117. "The Neuroscience of Leadership." *Strategy Business: International Business Strategy News Articles and Award-winning Analysis.* 30 May 2006. Web. <http://www.strategy-business.com/webinars/webinar/webinar-neuro_lead?gko=37c54>.

118. "The Neuroscience of Leadership." *Strategy Business: International Business Strategy News Articles and Award-winning Analysis.* Web. 10 Dec. 2010.

119. Nhau, Hanh, and Mai Vo-Dinh. *The Miracle of Mindfulness: a Manual on Meditation.* Boston: Beacon, 1987. Print.

120. Ohnsman, Alan, Jeff Green, and Kae Inoue. "The Humbling of Toyota." *Bloomberg Business Week* 22 Mar. 2010: 33+. Print.

121. "Pains and Pleasures of Social Life | Science/AAAS." *Science.* Web. 21 Dec. 2010. <http://www.sciencemag.org/cgi/content/summary/323/5916/890>.

122. Panzar, A., M. Viljoen, and J. L. Roos. "The Neurobiological Basis of Fear: a Concise Review." *South African Psychiatry Review* May (2007): 71-75. Print.

123. Paul, Richard, and Linda Elder. *Critical Thinking: Tools for Taking Charge of Your Professional and Personal Life.* Upper Saddle River, NJ: Financial Times/Prentice Hall, 2002. Print.

124. Pfeffer, Jeffrey. *What Were They Thinking?: Unconventional Wisdom about Management.* Boston, MA: Harvard Business School, 2007. Print.

125. Piattelli-Palmarini, Massimo. *Inevitable Illusions: How Mistakes of Reason Rule Our Minds.* Chichester: Wiley, 1996. Print.

126. Pitkin, Walter B. *A Short Introduction to the History of Human Stupidity*. New York: Simon and Schuster, 1932. Print.

127. Rand, Ayn. *Atlas Shrugged*. New York: Dutton, 2005. Print.

128. Ringleb, Al H., and Milan Pagon. "The CIMBA MBA Leadership Process." *NeuroLeadership Journal* Issue Two (2009): 42-52. Print.

129. Rock, David, and Linda J. Page. *Coaching with the Brain in Mind: Foundations for Practice*. Hoboken, NJ: Wiley, 2009. Print.

130. Rock, David, and Yiyuan Tang. "Neuroscience of Engagement." *NeuroLeadership Journal* Issue Two (2009): 15-22. Print.

131. Rock, David. "Managing with the Brain in Mind." *Strategy Business: International Business Strategy News Articles and Award-winning Analysis*. Web. 09 Dec. 2008. <http://www.strategy-business.com/article/09306?gko=5df7f>.

132. Rock, David. *Quiet Leadership: Help People Think Better—Don't Tell Them What to Do : Six Steps to Transforming Performance at Work*. New York: Collins, 2006. Print.

133. Rock, David. "SCARF: a Brain-based Model for Collaborating with and Influencing Others." *NeuroLeadership Journal* One (2008). *Www.NeuroLeadership.org*. NeuroLeadership Institute, 2008. Web. 2009.

134. Rosenberg, Jonathan B. *How Debuggers Work: Algorithms, Data Structures, and Architecture*. New York: John Wiley, 1996. Print.

135. Russo, J. Edward., and Paul J. H. Schoemaker. *Winning Decisions: Getting It Right the First Time*. New York: Currency, 2002. Print.

136. Schooler, Jonathan W. "Re-representing Consciousness: Dissociations between Experience and Metaconsciousness." *TRENDS in Cognitive Sciences* 6.8 (2002): 339-44. Print.

137. Schulz, Kathryn. *Being Wrong: Adventures in the Margin of Error*. New York: Ecco, 2010. Print.

138. Schwartz, Barry. *The Paradox of Choice: Why More Is Less*. New York: HarperCollins, 2005. Print.

139. Sibony, Olivier, and Dan Lovello. "Strategic Decisions: When Can You Trust Your Gut? - McKinsey Quarterly - Strategy - Strategic Thinking." *Articles by McKinsey Quarterly: Online Business Journal of McKinsey & Company. Business Management Strategy - Corporate Strategy - Global Business Strategy*. McKinsey & Company, Mar. 2010. Web.

140. Siegel, Daniel, and Debra P. McCall. "Mindsight at Work: an Interpersonal Neurobiology Lens on Leadership." *NeuroLeadership Journal* Issue Two (2009): 23-34. Print.

141. Slywotzky, Adrian J., and Karl Weber. *The Upside: the 7 Strategies for Turning Big Threats into Growth Breakthroughs.* New York: Crown Business, 2007. Print.

142. "Smeal Professor Addresses CEO Confidence and Risk-Taking — Research with Impact." *Research With Impact — Research with Impact.* Web. 18 Feb. 2010. <http://research.smeal.psu.edu/news/smeal-professor-discusses-ceo-confidence-and-risk-taking-in-speech>.

143. Smelser, Neil J., and Paul B. Baltes. *International Encyclopedia of the Social & Behavioral Sciences.* Amsterdam: Elsevier, 2001. Print.

144. Stone, Justin F. *Heightened Awareness: toward a Higher Consciousness.* Fort Yates, ND: Good Karma, 1989. Print.

145. "Strategic Decisions: When Can You Trust Your Gut?" *McKinsey Quarterly* (March 2010). Print.

146. "Stress: The Fight or Flight Response." *Psychologist World.com.* Psychologist World. Web. <http://www.psychologistworld.com/stress/fightflight.php>.

147. "Taking the Bias out of Meetings - McKinsey Quarterly - Strategy - Strategic Thinking." *Articles by McKinsey Quarterly: Online Business Journal of McKinsey & Company. Business Management Strategy - Corporate Strategy - Global Business Strategy.* Web. 10 Dec. 2010.

148. Taleb, Nassim. *Fooled by Randomness: the Hidden Role of Chance in Life and in the Markets.* New York: Random House, 2005. Print.

149. Taleb, Nassim. *The Black Swan: the Impact of the Highly Improbable.* New York: Random House, 2007. Print.

150. Taylor, Jim. "Prime Business: More to Fear than Fear Itself -Psychology Today." *Psychology Today. Psychology Today.* Sussex Publishers, LLC, 27 July 2009. Web. <http://www.psychologytoday.com/print/31387>.

151. Tedlow, By Richard. "Toyota Was in Denial. How About You? - BusinessWeek." *BusinessWeek - Business News, Stock Market & Financial Advice.* Web. 08 Sept. 2010. <http://www.businessweek.com/magazine/content/10_16/b4174076731775.htm>.

152. Thompson, George J., and Gregory A. Walker. *The Verbal Judo Way of Leadership: Empowering the Thin Blue Line from the inside up.* Flushing, NY: Looseleaf Law Publications, 2007. Print.

153. Tingling, Peter M., and Michael J. Brydon. "Is Decision-based Evidence Making Necessarily Bad?" *Slaon Management Review* Summer (2010): 71-76. Print.

154. Tobak, Steve. "Should 'Soft Skills' Be Key Executive Traits? | BNET." *BNET - The CBS Interactive Business Network.* 3 Jan. 2011. Web.

155. Tolle, Eckhart. *A New Earth: Awakening to Your Life's Purpose.* New York: Plume, 2006. Print.

156. "Toyota's Slow Awakening to a Deadly Problem." *The New York Times - Breaking News, World News & Multimedia.* Web. 08 Sept. 2010. <http://www.nytimes.com/2010/02/01/business/01toyota.html>.

157. Uleman, James S., and John A. Bargh. *Unintended Thought.* New York: Guilford, 1989. Print.

158. "Understanding Our Blind Spots—a Collaboration with The Wall Street Journal - MIT Sloan Management Review." *The New Business of Innovation - MIT Sloan Management Review.* Web. 16 Dec. 2010. <http://sloanreview.mit.edu/executive-adviser/articles/2009/1/5112/understanding-our-blind-spots/>.

159. Van Den Bos, Kees, and Joost Miedema. "Toward Understanding Why Fairness Matters: The Influence of Mortality Salience on Reactions to Procedural Fairness." *Journal of Personality and Social Psychology* 79.3 (2000): 355-66. Print.

160. Vandenbos, K., and E. Lind. "Uncertainty Management by Means of Fairness Judgments." *Advances in Experimental Social Psychology* 34 (2002): 1-60. Print.

161. Vandenbos, K., P. Poortvliet, M. Maas, J. Miedema, and E. Vandenham. "An Enquiry concerning the Principles of Cultural Norms and Values: The Impact of Uncertainty and Mortality Salience on Reactions to Violations and Bolstering of Cultural Worldviews." *Journal of Experimental Social Psychology* 41.2 (2005): 91-113. Print.

162. Warner, C. Terry. *Bonds That Make Us Free: Healing Our Relationships, Coming to Ourselves.* [Salt Lake City]: Shadow Mountain, 2001. Print.

163. Watts, Alan. *This Is It, and Other Essays on Zen and Spiritual Experience.* New York: Vintage, 1973. Print.

164. Wegner, D. M., and J. A. Bargh. "Control and Automaticity in Social Life." *The Handbook of Social Psychology.* By Daniel Todd. Gilbert, Susan T. Fiske,

and Gardner Lindzey. 4th ed. Vol. 1. Boston: McGraw-Hill, 1998. 446-96. Print.

165. Welles, James F. *Understanding Stupidity: an Analysis of the Unnatural Selection of Ideas, Beliefs and Behavior of Institutions and Organizations.* Greenport [N.Y.: Mount Pleasant, 2000. Print.

166. "What Is "The Art of Changing the Brain?"" *New Horizons for Learning.* May 2003. Web.

167. Wheatley, T., and D. M. Wegner. "Automaticity of Action, Psychology of." *International Encyclopedia of the Social & Behavioral Sciences* (2001): 991-93. Print.

168. Wiggins, Jerry S. *The Five-factor Model of Personality: Theoretical Perspectives.* New York: Guilford, 1996. Print.

169. Wilson, Timothy D. *Strangers to Ourselves: Discovering the Adaptive Unconscious.* Cambridge, MA: Belknap of Harvard UP, 2002. Print.

170. Winston, Robert M. L. *What Goes on in My Head?* New York: DK, 2010. Print.

171. Yarbus, A. L. *Eye Movements and Vision,.* New York: Plenum, 1967. Print.

172. Yeganeh, Bauback. *Mindful Experiential Learning.* Diss. Case Western Reserve University, 2006. Print.

173. Yontef, Gary, and James S. Simkin. "Gestalt Therapy: An Introduction." *The Gestalt Therapy Page.* Awareness, Dialogue, and Process Published by The Gestalt Journal Press, 1981. Web.

174. Zimmerman, M. "The Nervous System in the Context of Information Theory." *Human Physiology.* By Robert F. Schmidt and Gerhard Thews. Berlin: Springer-Verlag, 1989. 166-73. Print.

175. Zink, C. F. "Human Brain Appears "Hard-Wired" for Hierarchy, April 23, 2008 News Release - National Institutes of Health (NIH)." *National Institutes of Health (NIH) - Home Page.* Web. Winter 2008. <http://www.nih.gov/news/health/apr2008/nimh-23.htm>.

176. Zull, James E. The Art of Changing the Brain: Enriching Teaching by Exploring the Biology of Learning. Sterling, VA: Stylus Pub., 2002. Print.

Index

A

accuracy dimension, 70–71, 75, 83–86, 96, 130, 184, 186
actions, 39–40
acute stress response. *see* fight or flight response
adrenaline, 45
ambiguity, 46–47
amygdala, 44, 100, 171n26, 171n30, 199, 204
Ariely, Dan, 173n63, 210
assumptions error, 70, 74, 80, 96, 130, 184, 185
automaticity, 35–36, 101
awareness, corporate, 166–167
awareness index
    learning, 140–142
    mind-bug, 58, 115–117
awareness of group culture, 137

B

Barret, Justin, 203
Baumgarten, David, 208
behavioral economics, 210

behaviors, signs of mind-bugs and, 29–30
    see also reactive behavior
beliefs, 32n, 59
beliefs dimension, 70–71, 76, 87–90, 96, 131, 184, 187
blind spots, 132–133
blindness, competency, 70, 76, 89–90, 96, 131, 184, 187
brain
    hard-wiring of, 43–46, 102–103, 196
    hijacking of, 45, 85, 103–104
    mind and, 196
    psychiatry and, 197–198
    social status and, 207–208
    stimulus and, 202–203
    survival and, 36–37, 41
    understanding, 31
    see also mind
breakpoint, mental, 31, 60, 65–66, 109, 114, 119–120, 122, 137, 145, 149, 192, 196
bugs
    invention of term, 27–28
    software, 28
bureaucracy, status quo and, 19

C

Cannon, Walter Bradford, 170n17, 202
cellular and molecular neurobiology, 199–200
change, resistance to, 30
closed mind, 70, 76, 89, 96, 131, 184, 187
competency blindness, 70, 76, 89–90, 96, 131, 184, 187
competition, 166
conflicts, secret to resolving, 122–123
conforming error, 70, 77, 91–92, 96, 131, 184, 188
Conquest of Mind (Easwaran), 212–213
conscious processes, 38–39, 40
consciousness, corporate, 163–164
consistency, 162
context, 148–149
control, 46–47
corporate awareness, 166–167
corporate consciousness, 163–164
corporate environment, 18, 20
correction, 110, 111, 153–155, 189
cortisol, 45, 196
cosmology, 211
critical thinking, 211–212
Critical Thinking (Paul & Elder), 211–212

D

dACC, 206, 207
data favoritism, 70, 75, 85, 96, 130, 184, 186
data rejection, 70, 75, 85, 96, 130, 184, 186
debugging process, 147–152, 190, 192
decision construct, 149
decision making, process of, 33–34
decisions, 51–52, 145–146, 189, 196
see also debugging process
defensive reasoning, 126–127
defining the problem, 99–105
desires, 51
dimensions, 70, 71, 78, 95, 96, 184
disagreements, 122

E

Easwaran, Eknath, 212–213
Eisenberger, N. I., 205–206
Elder, Linda, 211–212
emotional attachments, 92
emotions, 50

exercises, 41, 47–48, 52–53, 58, 62–63, 78, 81–82, 85, 90, 93–94
see also awareness index
experience bias, 70, 76, 89, 92, 96, 131, 184, 187

F

fairness, 47
fear
    brain hijack and, 103–104
    description of, 44–45, 196
    neurobiology of, 171n25, 204
    Pavlovian conditioning and, 199–200
    role of, 99–100
    social, 45
    social threats and, 46–47
    see also fight or flight response
feedback, 142–143
feelings, 50–51
fight or flight response, 36, 44, 102, 104, 201–202
    see also fear; survival; threats
fighting the system, 19
filters, non-conscious, 35
Follett, Mary Parker, 173n61
foresight, 150–151
four dimensions, 70, 71, 78, 95, 184
    see also individual dimensions
free will, 211
functional magnetic resonance imaging (fMRI), 205

G

gathering and processing dilemma, 71, 88, 92
Gazzaniga, Michael, 202–203
generalization without evidence, 70, 75, 84, 96, 130, 184, 186
Gilovich, Thomas, 200–201
Goleman, Daniel, 171n30, 174n78
governance reforms, 23
Grand Design, The (Hawking & Mlodinow), 211
groups
    culture of, 137
    debugging process and, 190
    example regarding, 131–132
    improving interaction in, 110, 129–133, 189

mindlessness and, 136
survival and, 207
two ways and, 125–126
Groupthink, 92
gut instincts, 117–118

H

hands-on experience, 194
Hawking, S. W., 211
hiding weaknesses, 70, 77, 93, 96, 131, 184, 188
hijacking of brain, 45, 85, 103–104
hindsight, 150–151
Hopper, Grace, 27
How We Know What Isn't So (Gilovich), 200–201
Human (Gazzaniga), 202–203
human nature, 21, 29

I

improving interaction in groups, 110, 129–133, 189
improving learning and feedback, 110, 111, 139–143, 189
improving my own thinking, 110, 113–118, 189
infinite loop, 176n89
information processing, non-conscious, 34–37
informed leader fallacy, 10–11, 70, 74, 79–80, 92, 96, 130, 184, 185
Insel, Thomas R., 208
instincts, gut, 117–118
insula, 206

L

Langer, Ellen, 213–214
learning and feedback, improving, 110, 111, 139–143, 189
learning awareness index (LA Index), 140–142
LeDoux, Joseph, 199–200
Lieberman, Matthew D., 205, 206, 209
listening, 122

M

McDonald, Paul, 209–210
McHugh Paul R., 197–198
memory capacity, 101

mental breakpoint, 60, 65–66, 109, 114, 119–120, 122, 137, 145, 149, 192, 196
mind
always on, 38
brain and, 196
communications from, 52–53, 65
connections with, 37–38
definition of, 37
role of, 103
survival and, 41
see also brain
mind-bugs
avoiding, 14, 109, 136–137
awareness index for, 58, 115–117
concept of, 10
detecting, 11, 29, 31–32, 100
development of model of, 195–196
dimensions and, 70–71
eliminating, 12
evidence of, 17–18
identifying, 14
key condition for, 21
predicting, 102
predisposition to, 99–100
psychiatry and, 197–198
reactions to, 21
reference guide to, 73–77, 130–131
spiral of, 121
understanding, 13
see also individual mind-bugs
mindfulness, 55–58, 107–109, 110, 153–154, 159, 165, 190, 209, 213–214
mindlessness, 102, 107, 135–136, 155, 190, 214
see also closed mind
mirror neurons, 210
Mlodinow, Leonard, 211
mortgage crisis, 16

N

neurobiology, 199–200, 204
NeuroLeadership, 208–210
neuropsychology, 174n74, 202–203
neuroscience, 202–203
New Earth, A (Tolle), 213
non-conscious processes, 34–37, 38–39, 40, 101
norepinephrine, 202

O

office politics, 19
   see also corporate environment
organizational learning, 140
outcome attachment, 70, 76, 88, 90, 96, 99–100, 131, 184, 187

P

pain, social vs. physical, 205–207
Panzer, A., 204
Path to Better Decisions, 109–111, 123–124, 157–159, 189
pattern recognition. *see* seeing patterns that are not real
Paul, Richard, 211–212
Pavlovian fear conditioning, 199–200
   see also fear
Perspectives of Psychiatry, The (McHugh & Slavney), 197–198
physics, 211
point of view. *see* beliefs dimension
power insulation, 70, 77, 92, 96, 131, 184, 188
Predictably Irrational (Ariely), 210
Prius recall, 15–16
psychiatry, 197–198
psychology, 200–202, 212–214

Q

quiet space, 41

R

reactive behavior, 55–56, 107, 111, 135, 190, 196
   see also closed mind
readiness, 161–162
reflective behavior, 55–56, 58, 62–63, 107, 120, 190
   see also self-examination, objective; thinking
reflective thinking, 101–102, 105
reforms, governance, 23
regulations, 164–165
resistance, 162
risk, 23
Rock, David, 208
Roos, J. L., 204
rose-colored glasses, 70, 77, 92, 96, 131, 184, 188

S

Sarbanes-Oxley Act, 164
schadenfreude, 207
seeing patterns that are not real, 70, 75, 84, 96, 130, 184, 186
self-control, 209
self-examination, objective, 61–62, 65
   see also reflective behavior
shooting the critics, 70, 74, 81, 96, 130, 184, 185
shortcomings denial, 70, 76, 88–89, 92, 96, 131, 184, 187
Sibony, Olivier, 173n63
Slavney, Phillip R., 197–198
snap judgment defense, 70, 74, 81, 96, 130, 184, 185
social cognitive neuroscience (SCN), 204–208
social dimension, 70–71, 77, 91–94, 96, 131, 184, 188
social exclusion, 205–206
social fears, 45, 100–101
social status, 46–47
social threats, 46–48
"soft" skills, 31
source influence, 70, 74, 80, 96, 130, 184, 185
spirituality, 212–214
STAR model, 33–34, 39–40
state of mind, 110
status quo, 70, 77, 93, 96, 131, 184, 188
stimulus and response, 34, 104–105, 121, 125–126, 199, 202–203
stress, 21–22
structure, 18–19
sufficiency dimension, 70–71, 74, 79–82, 96, 130, 184, 185
survival
   brain and, 36–37, 43–44, 46, 103, 196
   fight or flight response and, 201
   groups and, 207
   hard-wired for, 10
   planning and, 38
   see also fight or flight response; threats
symmetry, 125, 127
sympathetic nervous system, 202

T

Takahashi, 207

taking command of thinking, 31, 59–63, 95, 108, 110, 120, 136–137, 162

Taylor, Jim, 201

thalamus, 199, 204

thinking
    critical, 211–212
    description of, 49–50
    exercise for, 52–53
    improving, 110, 113–118, 189
    poor habits of, 69–70
    taking command of, 59–63, 95, 108, 110, 120, 136–137, 162
    see also reflective behavior

30 second scan, 145–146, 191

Thomas, Gilovich, 32n

thought governance, 11, 165

thoughts, 49–51, 61, 108
    see also thinking

threats, 46–48, 100, 196, 201
    see also fear; fight or flight response; survival

threats, reaction to, 44

Tolle, Eckhart, 213

Toyoda, Akio, 15–16, 17n

Toyota, 15–18

trust, 47

two questions, 123, 125, 126–127, 136, 142, 154

two ways, 55–58, 107, 120–121, 127, 190

U

unverified information vs. fact, 70, 75, 83–84, 96, 130, 184, 186

V

ventral striatum, 206, 207

Viljoen, M., 204

W

wants. *see* desires

Williams, Kipling D., 205

NOTES

NOTES

NOTES

Set in Adobe Minion type
with ITC Officina Serif and Sans
Michael Höhne
Höhne-Werner Design
2012